THE
PURSUIT
OF
WHOLENESS

JOHN SQUIRES

THE PURSUIT OF WHOLENESS

WHAT IT MEANS TO BE TRULY HEALED

AN ALBATROSS BOOK

© John Squires 1995

Published in Australia and New Zealand by
Albatross Books Pty Ltd
PO Box 320, Sutherland
NSW 2232, Australia
in the United States of America by
Albatross Books
PO Box 131, Claremont
CA 91711, USA
and in the United Kingdom by
Lion Publishing plc
Peter's Way, Sandy Lane West
Oxford OX4 5HG, England

First edition 1995

National Library of Australia
Cataloguing-in-Publication data

Squires, John
The pursuit of wholeness: what it means to
be truly healed.

ISBN 0 7324 1047 9

1. Spiritual healing. 2. Healing – religious aspects.
3. Prayer – Christianity. 4. Prayer groups –
Christianity. I.Title.

248.32

Cover photo: John Waterhouse
Printed and bound by Griffin Paperbacks, Netley, SA

Contents

Preface

FROM THE MOMENT I SAT DOWN to write this book, a flood of memories began to fill my mind as I recalled some of the people and situations which have had an important influence on the development of my ideas and practices of healing. I became conscious, too, of the fact that I could not possibly recall them all and that, no matter how much I might like to thank them individually for the part they have played in this important area of my life, it would be impossible to do so for fear of leaving someone out. I can only hope that I have made my gratitude clear to them along the way.

For I have benefited enormously over the years from many friends and colleagues in Australia, England and the United States who have been willing to explore ideas and share experiences with me. I would like to thank them all, individually and collectively, for their generosity of spirit and graciousness in sharing their insights with me.

Just as importantly, however, I would like to thank all those who through the years invited me to be part of their lives by trusting me not only to listen to them in their pain, but also by taking my suggestions seriously, and allowing me to pray with them for healing. They have been able to teach me a lot, sometimes through bitter experience, and I am very grateful to them for giving me the privilege of being part of their lives. I would especially like to thank those who have given me permission to share something of their experience of healing with you.

Many of the stories in this book are those of individuals. In giving permission to use these stories, some have chosen to keep their own names, while others have changed the names and any details which might identify them without altering the substance of their stories in any way. At times, I decided to combine the experiences of more than one person into a single story where the details and circumstances were similar enough and a common problem was being spoken about in order to make it more widely applicable and to protect privacy. In every case, I have sought to respect the wishes of those involved in this regard. In this way, we have gained the benefit of their experience. However, no matter how we chose to do it, it was the hope of all that their story might help others in the pursuit of wholeness.

However, there is one story which does not appear in the book but which I would like to tell first. It is the story of how I began my own interest in healing. It is a story with a sad beginning and a sad ending, but a lot of joy in between.

Not long before I finished my university studies, some close friends of mine became parents for the second time. Unhappily, their daughter Chrissie suffered severe brain damage at birth due to lack of oxygen, and had to be cared for in a special hospital unit for some months before she was allowed home. My friends were devastated by what had happened and sought comfort and help in their need from the church to which they belonged.

Fortunately for them, there were a number of people in their church, including the minister, who were involved in a healing ministry. They encouraged them to seek help through prayer, which they did. In fact, while Chrissie was still in hospital, they started attending an evening healing service regularly mid-week, with the assistance of friends who helped with baby sitting. However, by the time Chrissie eventually came home, the arrangements which enabled them to benefit from the healing service no longer worked because one of them had resumed evening classes at university and the other was needed to look after the two children at home, especially as Chrissie required special care. They soon began to miss the support and encouragement they were getting from the healing service and, because of the pressure they were under, they were finding things very difficult indeed.

By that time I had begun my first full-time job and found that I could order my life a little differently than I had been able to do as a student. Therefore, I offered to look after the children so that my friends could resume attending the healing service from which they gained so much help. I must admit that I made this offer somewhat naively, more concerned about my friends' well-being than how I might cope with the baby-sitting. It proved to be quite a learning experience in more ways than one.

I soon discovered that a baby as severely handicapped as Chrissie required constant and extremely close supervision, and that it did not take much for an ordinary situation to become life-threatening. I can only assume that my friends' greater need for help made the risks involved in entrusting Chrissie to my care worth taking. However, as it turned out, we all ended up benefiting greatly.

My two friends would arrive home from their separate activities at roughly the same time and, over a cup of coffee, the one who had been at the healing service would share with us what she had learnt that night about prayer and faith in relation to coping with and overcoming sickness. At that time, there was a strong emphasis in that particular healing service on looking to God for answers to prayer and applying faith in practical situations. Much of this teaching was new to me at the time, and I found it fascinating. However, at no point did it remain in the realm of theory, as invariably I found myself in situations when left alone with Chrissie which forced me to put into practice what I had just learnt in order to avoid a potentially dangerous situation. To my delight, I found that the things I was learning had practical application in everyday life. I was beginning to learn through experience the connection between faith expressed through payer and changing circumstances, particularly in relation to healing. Put simply, it worked.

This went on for about eighteen months before my circumstances changed and I could no longer continue looking after Chrissie once a week and benefiting from this unique learning experience. However, by then I was thoroughly committed to the concept of healing through prayer and was keen to know more about the relationship of faith to healing and the interplay between the body and the mind in the healing process. I have spent a good part of my life ever since in these pursuits.

Sadly, Chrissie was never healed in a physical sense. In fact she died in 1992 at the age of twenty-five. Nevertheless, through prayer and faith, and through the loving care of family and friends over the years, she developed into a lovely young woman, able to live an independent and fulfilling life within the limitations of her severe physical handicaps and the requirements of the communal setting in which she spent her adult years. The joy which she radiated gave some indication of the measure of wholeness within, despite all outward appearances.

As a mark of my affection for Chrissie, I would like to dedicate this book to her. In a very real sense, she sparked my interest in trying to understand the nature of healing and inspired me to keep on in pursuit of wholeness.

I would like to thank my wife Barbara for her unfailing love and encouragement, my children, Kathryn and Martin, who have given me a great deal of support in getting on with the task of writing, and my secretary Judith who not only gave me valuable assistance when needed, but made me aware by her response to what I was writing that it was worthwhile making these ideas more widely available. I am indebted to them all.

Finally, I would like to say something about the way I approached the writing of this book. I was asked to write in a way which would make what I

have learnt about healing accessible to as wide a
group of people as possible. With this in mind, I
have tried to avoid religious jargon and to use terms
and expressions which give the meaning of what I
want to say without resorting to words which may
be unfamiliar to many or be overloaded with unfortunate and misleading connotations. I can only
hope that this approach will prove to be helpful, and
that those who miss the more familiar language they
might otherwise expect will try to understand why
it is not there.

Introduction

A MAJOR SHIFT IS TAKING PLACE TODAY in the way healing is understood and practised. Until recently, healing was almost the exclusive preserve of the medical profession which tended to view healing as the curing of physical or mental illness, usually by means of surgery, drugs, chemical intervention or other invasive means.

This limited view of healing is fortunately passing and with it the tendency for the treatment to be considered more important than the patient. This attitude sometimes resulted in the disease being cured, but not the patient. Perhaps this happened because the development of modern medicine necessitated a high level of concentration on scientific research, technology and the acquisition of sophisticated skills and techniques. Patient care was left largely to others, whose role in the healing process was often considered secondary.

In more recent times, there has been something of a backlash against this tendency of modern scientific medicine. While nobody denies the enormous contribution scientific medicine has made to healing or suggests that its role should be limited in any way, a balance between treating the complaint and treating the person is now thankfully returning. Some would say that it had never been lost, while others that it has been submerged in the sea of patients' expectations and a rapid advancement in the understanding and treatment of illness. Whatever the explanation, the return of this balance is accompanied by a greater willingness to consider some alternative and supplementary means of healing as legitimate.

In order to understand healing, it is necessary to look at the broad picture and understand that the *absence* of a treatable physical problem or distressing mental condition does not necessarily mean that a person is well. Healing is much more than the positive result of medical treatment. It may include that, but fundamentally it is a state of *well-being*, of wholeness. This is as much a feeling as a physical reality. This sense of wholeness is something for which most people long, even when there is no prospect of physical or mental cure. The path to healing, then, is very broad indeed. It includes traditional medical practice and much more besides.

Take the case of David. He came to a healing service I was conducting one evening. I had never met him before, so I knew nothing about him. He was obviously distressed and needed assistance in walking. As he knelt at the front of the church where people were being prayed for and received the laying-on-of hands which often accompanies healing prayer, I noticed that he began to cry. Later, he told me that as I placed my hands on him, he was filled with a great warmth.

At first, I took little notice of what was happening but, after a few moments when I had moved further down the line of those kneeling for prayer, I glanced back and was amazed to see him rise unassisted from where he knelt and walk back to his seat. A few weeks later, when I had got to know him better, David told me that he had been healed of a serious heart problem and severe pain in his legs that night. His doctor later verified the healing.

However, that wasn't the end of the matter for David. It appears that the tears he had experienced when prayed for at the healing service were related to a lifetime of trauma which was much more difficult to deal with than the physical problem. While the physical healing took place instantaneously, the inner healing which his physical problems had been masking took many more months of counselling and prayer.

There are many causes of distress, illness and death and many factors which contribute to a person's state of wholeness. Because of this, any meaningful definition of healing has to be broad enough to take into consideration cause as well as cure and recognise that, although humans are multi-faceted beings, healing must relate to the whole person and not just part of the whole. Although it may be described differently by others, I like to understand the whole person as made up of body, mind and spirit, and affected by relationships and environment. This is the background to all I do in promoting healing and helps me define what I mean by the term.

Healing contains elements of the known and the unknown, attitudes and feelings, the predictable and the unpredictable. To seek healing in the sense of being whole is to be open to all that can be legitimately offered as a result of human achievement and all that is possible through the intervention of God, and to allow those resources to affect every aspect of our lives, body, mind and spirit.

There are, of course, many valid contributions to the healing process. These include the traditional healing professions of the Western world, some modern adaptations of Eastern healing techniques, the various counselling schools that have developed from the researches of psychiatrists, psychologists and others, and the more intuitive counselling that has arisen over the past few years. Equally, there are many contributions to the healing process which must be seriously questioned and which may cause more harm than good, such as those based on various forms of mind control and self-delusion.

This greater tolerance of a wide range of healing techniques and remedies as complementary to traditional medicine, rather than in competition with it, has certainly given rise to some very strange and rather dubious practices. However, it has also allowed some acceptable alternatives to gain a new respectability.

Unfortunately, very few of these alternatives take the traditional spiritual values of the major Western religions seriously. This prevents many people in need of healing looking to those alternative approaches which may offer some legitimate help. Many of those approaches contain spiritual content which is alien and unacceptable to those from traditional Western backgrounds, or come as a 'package deal' which includes a philosophy they cannot agree with. This is particularly true for many Christians.

However, traditional spirituality is of great value in the healing process and opens up the possibility of healing in ways which are compatible with the faith of many ordinary people. Once people accept that their own spiritual beliefs and practices are important in the healing process, it gives them access to those alternative sources of healing which may benefit them, without requiring them to deny or compromise their faith or values in any way. It also enables them to use their faith in a way which has a positive effect on their whole being — and even gives them reason to hope for divine intervention in their lives.

The aim of this book, however, is not to criticise traditional medicine for its failure at times to understand and practise healing in a broader sense than that of curing various kinds of illness. Nor is the aim to examine the range of alternative techniques and remedies now available, or to evaluate those alternatives against traditional practices or religious beliefs.

Rather, this book aims:

❑ to highlight the importance of attitudes and feelings such as faith and hope in the healing process, and

❑ to encourage those in need of healing to look *outside* themselves to One whose power is greater than theirs, and to look *within* themselves for the inner resources which are there to promote their well-being.

These approaches, either separately or in combination, offer valuable assistance in the search for healing and need to be considered as complementary to the available medical resources and not in competition with them.

The value of faith in healing

There are many different ways of defining *faith*. When the word is used in relation to healing, it can mean simply an attitude or mindset which has its roots in a set of beliefs about God. Such faith enables those who have it to look outside themselves to One whose power is greater than theirs for help in time of need. They believe that God is able to influence the course of their lives, change their circumstances and bring them the desired help.

The amount of expectation they attach to this faith will vary according to the individual. However, the object of their faith, in the sense that the word is being used here, can be thought of objectively as an external power, or subjectively as a person. If thought of as a person, that person is usually referred to as God and is invested with varying characteristics, values and powers according to the different beliefs that individuals have about him.

I happen to believe in the Christian view of God whom I consider to be the only true God, knowable through Jesus Christ. Therefore, when I use the word 'faith' in relation to healing, I have the Christian view of God in mind as the object of my faith. However, it is also true that most of the aspects of faith which I describe in this book in relation to healing are effective, no matter what the object of faith happens to be. Various programs such as those run by Alcoholics Anonymous clearly demonstrate this fact, even though their concept of God is very broad indeed. The reason such a vague definition of God is so effective in these sorts of programs is because they are primarily talking about faith as an attitude.

There is no denying that such an attitude can have a remarkable effect on a person's physical, emotional and spiritual well-being. However, I believe that it is important to have a fuller concept of God than that if the attitude of faith is to be applied effectively to the healing process in such a way that it affects every part of our being. For instance, as a Christian, I believe that the God in whom I have faith sometimes intervenes directly in the lives and circumstances of people in response to prayer and brings about change for the better. When that happens, I call it a miracle because it has no rational explanation and can only be attributed to divine intervention.

In healing, faith is an attitude, expressed in prayer

and directed towards One who is considered to be greater than oneself and to have the power to heal. In this sense, faith looks outside of the self for help in time of need and is wholly dependent on the power of an Other. The One to whom prayer is directed is usually called God and is understood in accordance with one's own beliefs.

I happen to understand God in the Christian sense and to refer to him in the masculine — more for the sake of convenience than out of any desire to limit my understanding of him through gender. For me, faith is an important part of the way I relate to God generally and is absolutely vital when I pray for healing.

The value of hope in healing

While faith is an attitude which looks outside of the self, hope is an attitude which finds its power within. Hope — along with its opposite — hopelessness, is an attitude which has a high emotional component, and can affect a person's well-being in a positive or negative way.

Hopelessness can have such a profoundly negative effect that it can actually cause ill health and, in some cases, may even cause death. Hope, on the other hand, can have such a positive effect that it actually promotes well-being. For this reason, it is an important factor in the healing process.

However, hope is only one of a number of attitudes (mindsets) and emotions (feelings) which are increasingly seen as having a positive effect on the way the body responds to healing. In fact, the mind-body connection in healing is now taken very seriously indeed, as much by practitioners of traditional medicine as by those who practise alternative approaches to healing. No longer can the effect of attitudes and feelings be ignored in the healing process.

Hope is an attitude with a strong emotional content. It is found within us and it has the power, along with other emotions, to affect our well-being and to promote our healing. The emotions are very important when considering any approach to healing, but especially healing through prayer.

The reality of miracles in healing

Our attitudes and feelings are important, but they are only part of the picture.

The rate of development in medical science is so great and so amazing that we have become used to newspaper headlines proclaiming some new breakthrough. Almost every week, there is the announcement of some new wonder drug or miracle cure, the phenomenal development in the treatment of some life-threatening disease, distressing disability or major trauma, or the discovery of a revolutionary new preventative regime.

Such announcements excite our wonder and fill us with joy, especially when peoples' lives are saved or made more comfortable and pain-free as a result. We have grown used to hearing these things referred to as 'miracles' — which, of course, they are. They are wonderful deeds, wrought by human ingenuity for the good of humankind, and are all part of the great healing resource of modern medicine which is available to us.

However, despite all these advances, people still get sick and die. Sometimes that happens because there is no treatment available, sometimes because the treatment available cannot deal with the extent of the problem being faced. In fact, there are many situations where the medical resource can offer very little hope of healing.

Yet, despite this, most people know of healing which has occurred in such hopeless circumstances and which defies rational explanation. It may have happened to them personally or to someone close to them, or they have heard about it in some indirect way. The fact that so many people know of these sorts of situations suggests that unexpected healing still occurs and that we have every right to call these healings 'miracles' in the more traditional sense of being outside human control.

Such miracles are hard to explain rationally. Sometimes they can be linked to a particular lifestyle or belief system; sometimes we simply have to accept them as spontaneous remissions and leave it at that. However, there is a class of healing which is linked directly to prayer. These healings occur as a result of faith in God and cannot be overlooked by anyone interested in the healing process.

It is this type of healing which particularly interests me. However, the more I am involved in prayer for healing, the clearer it becomes that such healings are not usually as simple and straightforward as the stories about them often imply. Nor are there many certainties to offer when praying in this way.

Even miraculous healings of this sort occur in a variety of different ways. I have known people who have come for prayer and, without any preparation or counselling, have been healed instantly. Yet others, after a great deal of preparation, counselling and prayer, have found healing only after a long period of time or have only been healed in part. Others, it must be said, have never found healing at all, even though they have received the same attention as others.

Many people who seek healing through prayer do so because of a physical or emotional need. However, a presenting problem such as these will sometimes mask other unhealed areas of their life. When they find healing in the area that brought them to prayer in the first place, they are often encouraged by this to look for healing in those areas which had previously been hidden. Sometimes, the uncovering of these hidden needs becomes a more urgent matter for prayer and may even override the need for healing of the presenting problem as far as they are concerned.

However, no matter what the process, how long it takes or what it uncovers, whenever God is appealed to for help and healing results, I regard it as miraculous in the sense that God, whose power is greater than our own, has intervened to change the health or life of the person praying or being prayed for. This change is considered to be good by those who benefit from it and they usually respond by giving thanks to God for it.

I have no way of knowing exactly what caused David's physical healing when he came to our healing service that particular night. Nor do I know why others who were there were not healed in the same way. However, I do know that David, as desperate as he was, came with faith in God and with a strong desire to be healed which gave him great hope.

For David, faith and hope resulted in a miracle.

Such healings are not uncommon when people in need are prayed for. Prayer prayed by those who have faith in God and a strong positive attitude seems to be an effective way of enabling God's healing power to touch the life of those being prayed for, whether it is their own or someone else's.

Nevertheless, while we can learn from the stories of those who experience healing in this way, we need to be careful about drawing too many conclusions from them. We cannot explain completely why God intervenes directly in the lives of some to bring about the healing they desire, but only partly — or not at all — in the lives of others. The answer to this mystery may have more to do with the character of God than with the nature of prayer, even when that prayer is accompanied by faith and hope.

1

How healing involves the whole person

HEALING IS MUCH MORE THAN THE CURING of physical or psychiatric illness. Healing encompasses the whole person — body, mind and spirit — and results in a general sense of well-being. Healing in this sense comes in many ways, including by faith and hope.

ANN'S STORY OF WHOLISTIC HEALING

Ann is a good example of someone whose shattered life was restored because of this broad approach to healing. Like many others, she describes her healing as a miracle, not because it occurred in a completely inexplicable or spontaneous way, but because it came as a result of prayer and faith, together with the help of appropriate medical treatment, and because it ended up touching every area of her life —

body, mind and spirit. The end result of healing for Ann was an overall feeling of well-being which she had not had for many years.

❑ Ann's complex illness

I first met Ann when she was trying to deal with a number of family difficulties which had occurred in quick succession and combined to cause her world to fall apart. Her brother, to whom she was devoted, became seriously ill, she herself succumbed to a deep, depressive illness, and the problems in her marriage finally became intolerable. When it all became too much for her, she sought specialist medical treatment.

Before long, she was admitted to hospital and placed on heavy medication by her psychiatrist who was trying to do his best for her, though admittedly without much success. At the time, she was being treated primarily with drugs for a physical condition described in lay terms as a chemical imbalance in the brain. There was some suggestion that counselling might be helpful once she was stabilised by the right medication.

However, her condition was so bad that, although nobody could say for certain, the consensus of medical opinion was that she would spend the rest of her life on medication and would never be able to look after her family again in any meaningful way. It was conceded that she might eventually manage to do the family shopping again some time in the future, though only with assistance. This was not much of a prognosis for someone who was intelligent, well-educated, devoted to her family and used to living a very full life. Up until this time, Ann had a wide circle of friends and was actively involved in her local church. Now her life had literally fallen apart and nobody knew what to do about it.

Fortunately, Ann had faith. Her faith had certainly taken a battering over the years and was complicated by feelings of guilt. Nevertheless, in the end it was her faith which helped her find healing.

Ann's condition was so serious that when I first met her I had no idea how to relate to her. However, when she was released from hospital, I often noticed her walking past my office with her children. As she lived nearby, there was nothing unusual in this. Whenever I saw her, I made a point of greeting her, offering her support and assuring her of my prayers. After a while, this regular contact began to have an effect on her and several weeks later I was able to invite her into my office to talk, although at first she was able to do little more than cry.

When she felt safe in my presence, she eventually began to talk about herself. As her story unfolded, I quickly became aware that there was more to her illness than the chemical imbalance in the brain for which she was being treated and which was said to be affecting her emotional stability and relationships.

Ann's early life was one of rural poverty and emotional deprivation, which left her with a number of insecurities and a great need for love and approval. The poverty abated over the years, but the effect of the emotional deprivation remained. A wild youth, a teenage religious conversion, a number of relationships and an abusive marriage which failed to provide the emotional stability she craved left her even more insecure and full of guilt.

Like many abused people, Ann tended to blame herself for the problem. For years, nobody would believe her when she tried to speak about the abuse she was subjected to, preferring to believe that it was all in her mind.

Having to live with the nightmare of regular abuse and not being able to convince anyone that it was really happening, Ann began to doubt her own sanity and to assume that she was responsible for what was happening to her. That made her feel even more guilty. Even though she was able to attach some of the guilt she felt to things she had done and knew to be wrong within the context of her own value system, most of her guilt was an unconscious response to childhood conditioning. As a child, she was treated in ways which constantly made her feel guilty over the most trivial things. It was this unconscious feeling that left her vulnerable to abuse as an adult, exposed her to moral temptation and trapped her in a difficult relationship.

To add to her troubles, Ann had been exposed, during an extended time overseas earlier in her life, to aspects of a local religion which left her feeling fearful and controlled by it in a way that was difficult to explain. In fact, she thought she might be haunted or possessed by spirits associated with that particular religion. I had no way of knowing whether the reality behind this was psychological or spiritual. All I knew was that I had to treat it seriously because of the effect it was having on her.

Ann was in deep need. The years of abuse had left her feeling confused, guilty and insecure. However, even in this state, she somehow knew that all the influences on her life had combined to contribute to the position she was now in and that she had to find the sort of help that would not only deal with the symptoms of her problem, but also with its causes and the way in which all these different influences were interconnected.

She knew she needed a doctor to treat the physical aspects of her illness; a psychiatrist or counsellor to help her deal with the emotional trauma she had suffered; someone with spiritual understanding to help her deal with her guilt, remove herself from the moral temptations she faced, and overcome the fear and isolation of her life; and someone who had the skill to free her of any spiritual influences which might be robbing her of the love, acceptance and forgiveness which were an important part of her faith. She was in a real mess, but she was at least looking for the right sort of help.

In the times I spent with Ann, I soon discovered that she was suffering in every area of her life — physically, emotionally and spiritually — and that her relationships and ability to function satisfactorily were severely affected. If Ann was to have any real chance of a better life, all these areas had to be addressed in some way, for it seemed obvious that they were interconnected, even if at first I did not fully understand how.

Her healing would be very complex indeed.

❑ Ann's healing

Using the resources I had, and making it clear to Ann that she would not have to face the healing process alone because I and others would pray for her and support her as best we could, I sought to encourage her healing in the following ways:

a. *I encouraged her to continue with her medication* as I did not want to interfere with the medical treatment she was receiving. I knew full well that when she found healing, her doctors would withdraw the medication, because she would no longer need it. Remarkably, this happened a few months after she left her husband, although it took some time before she was strong enough to take that particular step.

b. *I encouraged her to work through the deep-seated emotional trauma of her life.* She did this by seeing a psychiatrist from time to time and by coming to me for counselling. I always made a point of praying with her before she went to the psychiatrist and of praying with her at an appropriate point during our counselling sessions, for I firmly believe in the power of prayer in every aspect of the healing process.

Although this took a long time and often proved to be painful, it had the effect of freeing her from the past and enabling her slowly to rebuild her emotional life.

c. *I encouraged her to look closely at her relationships,* especially those with her husband, parents and children, to gain some insights into how she was handling them and to explore alternative ways of doing so.

It was a long time before she was able to find any satisfactory solutions to her relationship difficulties. However, eventually she decided to step away from the one which she felt was causing her most harm, despite the emotional and spiritual pressures on her to remain.

From that time on, she began to relate to others differently. Because of the emotional healing that was taking place at the same time, she began to make decisions about her life, which made her feel better about herself.

d. *I also encouraged her to deal with the spiritual issues which were troubling her.* This meant strengthening her faith by rediscovering the power of love and forgiveness, and doing something about the on-going effects of the religious practices she had encountered overseas.

These had to be taken seriously, as they had left her fearful, subject to horrendous nightmares and feeling at the mercy of a spiritual power outside of her control. In a very real sense, she had to disconnect from a religious system which was causing her harm and reconnect with one she felt more comfortable with.

This spiritual journey proved to be as important for her healing as the other journeys she had embarked upon. In fact, in the end, they all turned out to be part of the same journey.

Ann's healing took a number of years and a great deal of anguish before it was over. The input needed was far greater at the beginning, but gradually tapered off. As the healing progressed during that time, Ann was able to cut back her medication until she came off it altogether. As already mentioned, this was linked to her decision to leave her husband — a decision which didn't come easily and took a long time to make.

It took months of medical treatment, counselling, prayer and support from a large number of people before she was strong enough to start making decisions about her life. It also included the difficult task of freeing her from the negative effects that her contact with the religion of another culture had had on her spiritual well-being.

When she came off the medication, her doctor, who found it difficult to accept the changes that had taken place, warned that she would probably need to go back on medication whenever a crisis came along. In fact, she hasn't needed to do so, despite the fact that there have been numerous crises in her life since that time.

As she got better, Ann upgraded her qualifications, succeeded in gaining a highly competitive job in a demanding profession, began to rebuild her relationships on a more satisfactory basis — and even form new ones — and regained her zest for life.

Although originally diagnosed as having a physical problem, her healing ended up touching every area of her life — body, mind and spirit — and brought her a new sense of well-being which she had not experienced for many years.

WHAT ISSUES ANN'S STORY RAISES
This story will raise different issues for each of us.
Here are some it raises for me:

❑ **First, Ann's story is a healing miracle**
When the unexpected occurs as a result of prayer as
in this case, it rightly deserves to be called a *miracle*.
However, it has to be admitted that there are some
approaches to healing which employ a form of faith
more closely identified with hypnosis and mind
control than faith in the more traditional sense of
trusting God. Many so-called faith healers use techniques and deceptions to harness the power of the
mind to bring temporary relief to sufferers without
achieving any long-term benefits.

These approaches need to be avoided by those
seeking healing because of the harm they do and
because of the way they exploit those in need. Faith
as a healing dynamic is a component of many belief
systems, though care has to be exercised when
choosing between them. Any legitimate use of faith
for healing must include a genuine openness to God
and must not make extravagant claims or raise false
expectations.

❑ **Second, Ann's story suggests that**
   traditional medicine is not enough
As I have listened to the stories of those who have

come for prayer in the way she did, and read widely over the years, I have come to the conclusion that there are always some for whom traditional medical practice has very little to offer apart from palliative care. There can be many reasons for this, the main ones being that there is no effective treatment available, or that the usual treatment has had little or no effect in their particular case, despite all reasonable expectation to the contrary. Even those whose illnesses respond to medical or surgical intervention can sometimes be left feeling just as unwell after the treatment as before it began.

Many who find themselves in this situation look for alternative ways of completing the job. Thankfully, an increasing number are turning to God in prayer for this and, by doing so, are avoiding some of the unfortunate consequences resulting from less scrupulous alternatives.

This does not mean that there is anything wrong with traditional medicine as such, even though there are those within the medical profession who are aware of its limitations and are gradually exploring ways of broadening its approach to healing to include the whole person. However, it does explain why there is such an upsurge of interest in alternative medicine and a greater willingness to acknowledge the influence of the mind on the way the body functions, both in sickness and in health. All of this has coincided with a growing awareness of the spiritual aspects of life and the way they, in turn, influence the healing process.

As a result, those who are sick or in need of healing in some area of their life are now more likely to be treated as a whole person rather than a person with a diseased part or a particular illness. The development of holistic medicine is evidence of this change of approach. Moreover, we now find that the beliefs and attitudes of a person are generally taken more seriously in the healing process.

One woman I know was treated quite dismissively when she openly expressed her belief that faith in God would see her through the operation she was facing. Ten years later, on returning to hospital for the same operation, she was actively encouraged to believe in God for healing as well as to trust in the skill of the surgeons. Her faith was now acknowledged as vitally important in her healing, whereas ten years previously it had been dismissed as irrelevant.

❑ Third, Ann's story suggests the inter-relatedness of all aspects of a person

The belief in such inter-relatedness is now widely acknowledged. Healing is no longer understood only in terms of curing physical or psychiatric illnesses, but rather as relating to the whole person. It is now generally recognised that a problem in one area of life may have an effect on other areas as well. Therefore, despite all the wonderful advances in medicine over the past few centuries which undoubtedly save lives and alleviate pain and suffering in remarkable ways, there is often a sense that something is missing, that the healing is not complete.

This may be due to the scientific approach of modern medicine which has by necessity concentrated more on the parts than the whole. Or it may be due to the high expectation which the non-medical community has placed on medical practice to produce a sense of well-being, only to be disappointed when it doesn't occur.

Whatever the reason, a growing disillusionment on both sides has had the positive result of broadening the approach to healing in such a way that it is now understood to include the effect of the mind and the spirit on the body.

A senior medical practitioner once confided in me: 'We doctors cannot heal anybody. We can only create the conditions for healing to take place.'

I am not sure how far others would agree with this statement about the healing process, but without denigrating the skills of doctors and the advancement of scientific medicine, it does give a different perspective on healing. An acknowledgement of the healing power of the body itself in this way highlights the fact that healing is the result of many interrelated factors and that there may be many other ways than modern scientific medicine by which the conditions for healing to take place may be created. Some of these ways may lie within us and some of them outside of us.

❑ Fourth, Ann's story suggests the part faith can play in healing

While there can be no denying that Ann's healing touched every area of her life and was contributed to by many different people, its effectiveness can be attributed directly to her faith and to the faith of others. Without this added dimension of faith, her healing may not have occurred to the extent that it did.

It was certainly through faith that many of the difficult causes of some of her problems were able to be dealt with successfully, especially those of a spiritual nature. Ann's faith also enabled her to resolve some of the childhood experiences through forgiveness, which is a very important aspect of her relationship with God.

Because of her faith, Ann never lost hope and her healing ended up touching every part of her being — body, mind and spirit — and brought change to her relationships and physical environment in profound ways.

It was really quite a miracle.

2

What true healing is

IN RECENT YEARS, there has been a growing acceptance by the general community of alternative medicine, coinciding with an enormous increase in the number of its practitioners. This growing interest in holistic medicine, in some areas rivalling conventional medicine, has been due to four factors:

- ❑ partly to a reaction to the scientific approach of modern medicine,
- ❑ partly to the rise of alternative healing practices,
- ❑ partly to a natural development in the quest to understand human nature, and
- ❑ partly to a resurgence of interest in mysticism and spirituality generally as part of our post-modern age.

As a result, we are now able to redefine what we mean by health and healing and to look beyond the traditional sources of healing as the only means of bringing it about.

Ann's story, as I indicated in chapter 1, is a great reminder that we are much more than the sum of our parts. We are whole beings, not just separate bits and pieces functioning in isolation from one another, and true healing can only occur when a person is considered as a whole. This is not a new revelation, but one which has persisted down through the ages, despite the tendency in more recent centuries for it to give way to the ascendancy of scientific medicine which has tended to concentrate on the parts rather than the whole.

Over the years, I have found it helpful to have the following definition in mind when I seek to encourage healing in people's lives:

Healing means being at peace with God, at peace with oneself, at peace with others, and at peace with the world.

The ideas contained in this definition are not easy to put into practice. Nevertheless, it is worth doing so, because in the end such ideas will produce a sense of well-being far beyond the curing of physical illness. This definition of healing is about wholeness and, if we want to travel the path of true healing, we need to understand it more fully.

HEALING MEANS PEACE WITH GOD

It is an amazing fact that a vast majority of people around the world still express some belief in God despite the modern world's commitment to science and technology and the efforts of many philosophers over the years to discourage it. Even though the way in which different people understand and define God may vary, it would appear that belief in God in some form is fundamental to our human nature. Many would say that this is because we are as much spiritual beings as we are physical and emotional ones. If this is the case, then people have to be true to their beliefs and at peace with their understanding of God if they want to be whole.

Most of those who express belief in God seem ready to accept that God has power over their lives, whether real or imagined, and they are usually ready to turn to God for help, particularly in time of need. Many explanations are offered for this phenomenon by philosophers, psychologists, anthropologists and theologians. All I want to do here is to note it and suggest that its importance for our general sense of well-being cannot be underestimated.

The Bible, one of the major religious documents in the world, explains this universal spirituality by claiming that human beings are made in the image of God. This seems to suggest that all human beings have the stamp of God upon them or the spirit of

God within them. It is this spirit 'within' which longs to connect with the divine Spirit, or maybe even to *dis*connect from it — for both these desires are really part of the same human process which takes us either closer to or further away from God. Both are reactions to our innate spirituality and are likely to have a large emotional component to them — as we shall see later.

If we humans, then, have a spiritual dimension to our lives and are more than just the sum of our parts, it follows that any disturbance within our spirit is likely to have an effect on the rest of our being. The spiritual dimension of our lives has to be considered just as seriously as any other when we are seeking healing or wholeness, for it means that we can look to spiritual resources such as faith, which can have a profound effect on healing.

This effect can result from a positive attitude within, or from miraculous intervention by a power which is both outside of and greater than ourselves. Faith, hope and the desire for a miracle all need something or someone to focus on to be effective. Some people find that something within themselves; others outside themselves. When it is found outside of the self, it is often referred to as God and invested with great power.

However, it is not necessary to view God in such an objective way and many of the world's great religions, including Christianity, have a much more personal view of God than that. The Christian view of God, for instance, includes the idea that God was involved in the creation of the world in some way and that he continues this involvement by sustaining it and caring for every part of it, including humanity. As a result, Christians tend to relate to God in a personal way and understand him as being interested in them and able to help them. They tend to use images such as that of a good father and his child to describe this spiritual connection with God.

Many of the people whose stories I tell in this book became aware of the need to include the spiritual dimension of their life in their search for healing. Finding peace with God was very important for Ann, for example, who is a Christian. Without God to turn to, she would not have had the faith or hope to believe for change in her life. In order to believe for change and to hope for the future, she needed to be at peace with God. She found that peace through forgiveness, love and the supportive friendship of those who felt the same about God as she did.

Peace with God is vitally important for our well-being and cannot be ignored in the healing process.

HEALING MEANS PEACE WITH SELF

It doesn't take a great deal of understanding of human nature to realise that many people are not at peace with themselves. The growing awareness of the effect of childhood trauma, especially in the area of physical, emotional and sexual abuse, has highlighted the extent of the problem and the legacy it has left behind. However, this is only one of a number of possible causes of inner disturbance which people bring with them into adult life and which may cause distress.

Different experiences affect people in different ways and it is often hard to predict how people will respond to the things which happen to them. We know that the emotions play a vital part in the way we cope, so the healthier the emotional upbringing we have had, the more likely we are to handle the traumas of life in a reasonably healthy way. However, if a person has not had a healthy emotional upbringing and inner hurts from the past remain unresolved, we know that these hurts can have a profound effect on their emotional and physical well-being in the present. For the past will always go on affecting the present to some extent until it is satisfactorily resolved or we have learnt to cope with its effects on our present life in appropriate ways.

The healing process needs to take this into account and deal with any unresolved emotional scars or hurts from the past which may be having an effect on the present. This is as important as tackling the presenting problem if true healing it to be fully experienced. It has to be remembered, however, that there are many ways of going about this and that not every problem needing healing has an underlying emotional cause. It is always best to start with the presenting problem and see what happens. If there is an underlying emotional cause it will eventually surface in some way and become obvious.

I have already explained how significant it was for Ann to deal with the past in order to be healed. Her childhood experiences had left her emotionally damaged and vulnerable in her adult life. It was only as she was able to get in touch with the feelings of worthlessness and hopelessness that were buried deep inside her — and go through the pain associated with the resolution of those feelings — that she was able to rebuild her emotional life in a satisfactory way and find peace within.

Ann's story is not unique. Most of us have some area of our inner life with which we are not at ease. We don't always recognise what it is or acknowledge it, even though others may see it in us because of the way it affects our relationships and behaviour. It is often only when confronted with the honesty of others or a growing self-awareness that we have the courage to admit that something is wrong and then deal with it.

The hurts I am talking about are not necessarily from the distant past. They may relate to a recent trauma. Increasingly, the link between trauma and sickness is being recognised and treated as part of the whole problem. Therefore, whether it is recent trauma or past hurts, the interaction between the emotional and the physical — the mind and the body — is well documented and the subject of on-going research. It is already beginning to influence medical treatment and lies behind many of the alternative healing practices which are growing up or being revived at present. Needless to say, it cannot be ignored when seeking the sort of healing which brings wholeness and not just the curing of a physical illness.

If the physical problem has been caused or exac-erbated by emotional hurts or traumatic events, there will be no long-term solution by ignoring them and by treating only the physical problem. Every aspect of a person's life has to be considered when seeking to bring healing to that person: the medical, the emotional, the spiritual. The growing amount of literature now available on holistic medi-cine is testimony to the growing orthodoxy of this position on healing. It is an extremely important understanding to have when praying for someone to be healed.

To enjoy the sort of healing which leads to a greater sense of well-being, there needs to be peace within.

HEALING MEANS PEACE WITH OTHERS

Ann's story shows very clearly the effect that a difficult relationship can have on a person's physical and emotional well-being. However, there are many other dynamics in relationships which may also have to be considered when seeking healing.

For instance, we are much more aware these days of the destructive influence of co-dependency in relationships because of the way it limits the integrity and potential of those caught up in it. It is not hard to see how people get trapped in such relationships and how those involved collude with each other in order to keep themselves trapped. The hidden cost of suppressed emotions in relationships, whether they are abusive, co-dependent or dysfunctional in some other way, can be seen by the way those caught up in them feel about themselves and relate to others.

Unresolved problems in relationships which result in the emotions being suppressed can also lie behind physical illness or be part of it. Resentment, anger and hatred are just some of the emotions which can be suppressed in this way. If left unresolved, these emotions are often expressed inappropriately and may affect not just relationships, but a person's general sense of well-being as well.

I shall never forget the man whom I spoke to after a healing service I once conducted. When I asked what his problem was, he said: 'I was dying of resentment.' He had actually had cancer but, through counselling and help from his doctors, he had come to believe that the cause of his illness was the resentment he felt towards his brother as the result of a rift in their relationship many years before. As he was helped to understand this and find ways of restoring the relationship through forgiveness and reconciliation, he went into remission and enjoyed a number of happy, fulfilling years when, according to the original prognosis, he should have been dead because of the way the cancer had spread throughout his body at the time.

This remarkable story of healing has to be balanced by that of the elderly woman who could only be described as pickled in her own bitterness. Her long-held hatred of her sister somehow sustained her through numerous illnesses, even though she never seemed to enjoy anything in life except hating others. In this case, her bitterness and hatred somehow had a preservative effect on her body. However, I never thought of her as a whole person, even though she managed to hold onto life so tenaciously. She was physically well, but emotionally crippled. She had no meaningful relationships with anyone.

Peace with others is a major component of our well-being. It is to be actively pursued if we are to enjoy the sort of healing which brings wholeness.

HEALING MEANS PEACE WITH THE WORLD

When I talk about being at peace with the world, I am not just talking about those big issues over which individuals have little control even though they may have a profound effect on their life. My primary concern here is not with pollution, global warming, population growth, the wide use of chemicals in agriculture and the deterioration of the urban environment in many parts of the world. Nor is it with those aspects of employment and living conditions which are largely determined by others.

I am more concerned, in the context of healing prayer, with those things over which we *do* have some control and which we can choose to do something about if they are harming us. These would include the type and amount of food we eat, the substances we ingest, the types of entertainment and leisure activities we engage in, the lifestyle we choose to follow and the influences we subject ourselves to, whether we fully understand the effect they have on us or not.

I would not deny that basic needs such as food, water, adequate shelter and elementary hygiene are major problems for a large portion of the world's population and have to be addressed globally in order to find just solutions to meet those needs. However, while most of as in the West have our basic needs met, there are often many aspects of our individual environment which cause illness and distress and which we can do something about if we see the importance of it for our well-being.

Environmental health is a growing concern, especially amongst those who work with the poor and disadvantaged, but it is not confined to these groups. It is a relevant issue for all of us, especially since it can have a profound effect on our health. There are many aspects of our environment which obviously cause distress, but there are others which are less obvious, such as noise pollution, the pressures of everyday living and the unrealistic demands of some employers. All of these can cause or contribute to illness in individuals or rob them of a sense of well-being. They cannot be ignored in the quest for healing.

It is now well recognised that there is no point in curing the illness, or solving the problem and then sending the patient back to an old environment and well-established behaviour patterns which caused the sickness in the first place, without trying to do something about them. That is why so much effort is going into public health campaigns and programs which address the causes of problems rather than merely treating the illnesses themselves.

The same is true of healing generally. If we concern ourselves only with the presenting problem, whether it be physical, emotional or even spiritual, what we're left with when the problem is solved is a 'sickness-shaped' hole. If all that surrounds that hole is not changed, then the problem will come back to fill it up, even if some limited form of healing has taken place.

To bring about that change, we may have to address the bigger issues, either by coming to terms with them and learning to live with them, or by trying to do something about them. More immediately, however, we may have to look closely at ourselves and face the possibility of changing our lifestyle or our immediate environment.

This may mean dealing with loneliness or finding another job. It may mean making decisions which affect whatever caused the problem in the first place or contributed to it in some way — such as lifestyle, diet, stress or even physical location. It will be different for everyone, for everyone's circumstances are unique. Individuals will have to decide for themselves whether the things which surround their sickness or problem need changing in order for them to find healing. If so, then they will need to do something about their personal environment, or they may unwittingly rob themselves of the healing for which they long.

I have already shown how important this was for Ann. In order to find healing, she had to change her lifestyle, physical location and the things to do with her relationships which kept her trapped in her illness. It was only as she made the changes necessary to prevent the illness returning that she began to experience complete healing. Ann changed the sickness-shaped hole in her life by giving it new surroundings, a new environment. In this way, she not only prevented an easy return for the problems she was dealing with, but made sure her healing would continue on to wholeness.

She found peace with a world which had previously worked against her and in the process she began to enjoy a new sense of well-being. Peace with the world is an important, though often overlooked, part of our healing.

Healing, then, is about wholeness. It's not just about the curing of physical illnesses or resolving emotional problems. It is about the whole person — body, mind and spirit — and about the sense of well-being which results from the way we relate to God, ourselves, others and the world.

3

When healing that defies reason takes place

HOW ARE PRAYER AND FAITH related to healing? To discuss this relationship adequately, we need to accept the possibility that the unexpected sometimes occurs during the course of an illness, resulting in a healing which is contrary to all expectation. When this happens, it is often referred to as a spontaneous remission, though sometimes it is called a miracle.

There is some reluctance by medical authorities to call an unexpected healing of this sort a miracle — 'spontaneous remission' is a term more likely to be used by them. I once asked a senior surgeon when he would describe a long-term spontaneous remission as a healing miracle. He replied that he never would, not even if the healing lasted the rest of the life of the person involved and no explanation was ever found for it.

This, of course, is an extreme position. Others are more generous in their assessment and will often refer to a long-term spontaneous remission as a miracle in order to explain it, even if they have no particular belief system to fit it into themselves.

For our purpose, it doesn't really matter whether we call such healings miracles or spontaneous remissions, as long as we allow the possibility for the unexpected to happen when we pray for healing and look to God for it when we do so. The evidence of miracles which have come as a result of prayer and which cannot be explained by ordinary means is all around us. Prayer for healing which results in healing is usually linked to the faith of those praying.

When unexpected healing is linked to prayer and faith, it is right to refer to it as a miracle and acknowledge that it has occurred through the intervention of an outside power. That power is usually, though not exclusively, associated with God in some way. It is this association between God and miracle through the medium of prayer and faith which causes difficulty for some and gives encouragement to others in their search for healing. The possibility of a miracle is one of the options open to us in the broad spectrum of healing resources available to those in need.

Miracles of healing occur both in medical and religious settings. It is not unusual to hear of miracles in a medical setting either during the course of ordinary medical treatment or by extraordinary means. In this setting, the word 'miracle' is generally used to describe something which has a scientific explanation, even if it goes beyond the bounds of usual expectation.

However, when the healing defies scientific explanation, it can only be attributed to chance or to the intervention of a power greater than the power of those involved in the healing process. If we opt to explain such healings by chance, we are locked into fatalism. However, if we opt to explain them as the intervention of a power outside the self, we can legitimately ask how we might access that power and become the beneficiaries of it. As soon as we do this, we are really asking questions about prayer and faith, for these are the spiritual means available to us to relate to God who is the repository of that power and ask for his help. This suggests that the intervention of God in the lives of those in need is not random, but occurs in response to prayer and faith.

There are many people who are living examples of the reality of miraculous healing occurring as a result of prayer and faith. These people have recovered from life-threatening conditions and been free of their problem for the rest of their lives, even though they were expected to die or suffer chronic disability as a result of it. They are an inspiration to the rest of us never to give up hoping for a miracle when faced with a similar need.

We can learn a lot from the experience of those who have found healing through prayer and faith, though we must be careful when doing so not to imply that there are certain ways of praying which guarantee a successful outcome.

ROSEMARY'S STORY OF HEALING

Rosemary and her husband are old friends of mine. I first met Rosemary when she was pregnant with their fourth child and extremely ill with kidney damage. Her condition was serious enough for me to be asked to pray with her and offer what support I could.

Happily, all went well and she gave birth to a healthy baby boy. She recovered well and continued to live a full and satisfying life.

❑ Rosemary's physical decline and diagnosis

Soon afterwards, Rosemary became pregnant again. Several months later, the opportunity arose for she and her husband to travel to New Zealand with a number of others, including myself, for a conference. This included some inspirational teaching and practical instruction on prayer and faith.

Although Rosemary was not considered a suitable traveller because all her pregnancies had been complicated by renal damage, she decided to make the journey. All went well until the night before she and her husband were to return home. She went into premature labour and, after a breech delivery, gave birth to a baby girl. Neither Rosemary nor the baby came through the birth unscathed.

Just prior to our departure from New Zealand, Rosemary's husband rang to inform us how desperately ill Rosemary and the baby were and to ask us to pray for them. Although we had very little information to go on, we felt encouraged by what we had learnt at the conference and by our own prior experience of praying in faith for healing to pray that Rosemary and the baby would be healed. We later learnt that the little baby had died after five days. Rosemary, however, had come through the ordeal and miraculously survived a series of medical complications which many expected would claim her life.

In hospital, Rosemary had sunk into heart failure which went undetected because it was masked by kidney failure and pneumonia. She was also suffering anaemia. Despite her condition, she was allowed out of hospital in time for the baby's funeral. The church which Rosemary and her husband belonged to flew one of their pastoral workers to be with her during this time. The pastoral worker also happened to be a close friend of Rosemary's and was able to give her the additional support and comfort she needed as well as pray with her about her continued ill-health.

After a short return to hospital and under close supervision by the local doctor, Rosemary's health improved marginally. Finally, after many anxious weeks of waiting, she was allowed to fly home. However, even then, her main problem had not been diagnosed, let alone treated.

The joy of being reunited with her family and the optimism she felt at being well enough to fly home soon gave way to anxiety when a doctor on a routine visit found her gasping for breath and offered to do some tests. They revealed that Rosemary's lungs were barely functioning and that she had an enlarged, shapeless and waterlogged heart. Her blood tests were disquieting as well.

She was immediately admitted to the intensive care unit of her local hospital and was visited by the cardiac consultant who advised her to remain in hospital for observation and treatment. Privately, he warned her husband that kidney disease together with pulmonary embolism and heart failure gave little scope for treatment or little hope of recovery.

Rosemary and her husband now acknowledged a truth which they had not guessed at before, despite all that had happened: her life was in danger.

Stunned by this realisation, they exhausted all they needed to say to each other at that time, then acted in a way which was consistent with their beliefs: they read a psalm from the Bible and a page from a collection of devotional comments by a well-known preacher of the nineteenth century. Then they prayed together.

Strangely, the devotional comments they read concerned the parents of Samson, an Old Testament character, who were petrified after being visited by an angel sent from God. Despite their fear, Samson's parents concluded that God could not have meant to kill them after speaking to them in this way.

This off-beat incident gave enormous courage to Rosemary and her husband as they faced the awesome possibility of Rosemary's death and they felt fortified in their faith by the possibility that God did not want her dead, when he had dealt with them the way he had up to this point. She was well-prepared for death herself, but not for the impact it would have on her family.

The next day, she was visited by a sorrowful procession of close family members and friends who had come to bid their farewells. Now on oxygen, she felt considerable relief, even though the heart monitor continued to reveal the complete disarray inside her body.

❑ Rosemary's slow road to miraculous recovery

In order to cope with the negative impact of what

the monitor was telling her, Rosemary did an extraordinary thing. She covered the monitor screen with get-well cards. This simple action proved to be a turning point.

This action may have been a symbol of her faith, or an attempt to block out the continually negative reinforcement of her condition which the heart monitor screen represented. Whatever it was, it coincided with a change in her overall condition. Within a few days, her breathing had improved and her heart rate, though still highly irregular, had slowed significantly. She had confronted her condition with positive faith and changes began to occur.

Her doctor was delighted with these inexplicable changes and had her moved from the intensive care unit back to a medical ward. This move was accepted by Rosemary as a definite sign of hope. Over the following week, with renewed faith and hope for the future, she began to walk again, shower and practise sitting up, even though it left her feeling very tired.

The medical specialists now accepted that she would live. However, they warned her that, even with all the improvements possible in her condition, the enlargement of her heart muscle meant that she would probably never be able to undertake any substantial activity again.

Despite these warnings, her attitude of faith remained firm, her hope was sustained and improvement in her health continued. After three weeks, she was released from hospital on medication and under close supervision. Once again she was warned that this regime would have to continue for the rest of her life. A month later, however, Rosemary was managing by herself and, against all expectation, her heart had returned to its normal size and function.

This can only be called a miracle.

❑ Rosemary's healing as seen by her supporters

In order to explain the background to this miracle, I need to add that throughout the entire time of Rosemary's illness, there had been constant prayer for her by a wide circle of family and friends.

All those who prayed for her believed that God was able to intervene in her life and change her physical condition and hoped beyond all expectation that he would do so. Prayer with faith such as this, reinforced by an emphasis on positive attitudes, was an extremely important part of Rosemary's healing.

At no point in her illness did Rosemary or those who were praying for her deny the reality of what was happening or act recklessly in regard to her treatment. Their faith at all times was directed towards God whom they knew from experience was capable of intervening and whom they trusted to act favourably towards Rosemary. They knew that they could not determine the outcome of their prayers by bargaining with God or by praying according to a set formula. However, because of the nature of their faith, they never doubted that good would result from their prayers.

In order to maintain their faith, they found it important to look beyond the present reality of the sickness to the healing which they hoped would come. I have no doubt that each person found their own way of doing this. Some, I know, chose to have in mind an image of Rosemary well and functioning normally as they prayed. This helped them concentrate on the positives and eliminate negative thoughts and attitudes from their prayers. Rosemary did this more graphically by blocking out the screen of the heart monitor.

However they chose to do it, it was important for those praying for healing to have faith to look beyond the present circumstances of her illness to what they were hoping for, to eliminate negative thoughts and attitudes from their prayers so that they could deal with doubt and concentrate on faith, and to trust God with the outcome, without thinking they could control it.

Nobody would suggest that praying like this is easy. However, it was the way that those who were praying for Rosemary prayed at the time and I have no doubt that, to a person, they would attribute Rosemary's healing to God's goodness in choosing to intervene in her life in the way he did, and not to their effort.

Prayer and faith were important in Rosemary's healing, but in the end it came from God.

PRAYING FOR HEALING IN A WAY
THAT IS NOT APPROPRIATE

Prayer is one of the great spiritual disciplines of most of the major world religions. It has many different aspects — including petition, which is particularly important for healing. Those who pray for healing perceive prayer as the link between themselves and the One to whom they pray — and whom they believe has the power to intervene in their lives.

Now this in itself is not wrong. However, many organised belief systems seek to formalise this link by turning prayer into something mechanical. This can lead either to a *fatalistic* view of prayer, where the outcome is left purely to chance, or a *mechanistic* one, where the results are seen as dependent on the way in which the prayer is carried out. Neither is desirable — least of all the one which assumes a world view based on fate. However, the mechanistic view of prayer is the one more likely to be adopted by those who pray for healing, especially if they are uncomfortable with uncertainty. For it implies a direct link between the correct way of praying and receiving the desired answer.

Unfortunately, as with all prayer, there are a number of variables in the mechanistic approach which may affect the outcome. These variables include the length of the prayer, the number of times it is prayed, the suitability of the person praying, or the formula being used. The emphasis on using a correct formula, such as 'Lord, I *believe* you are healing this person *now*', or on taking a 'name-it-and-claim-it' approach is seen as particularly important. However, when the answer doesn't come, the presence of these variables ensures that any lack of 'success' can be attributed to human failure. There is plenty of room for human rationalisation.

This avoids the inconvenience of having to say that there may be something wrong with the approach being used or (a worse option) that God may not wish to respond. It assumes that God always heals if we can only get the formula right; therefore, there must be some other reason why God has not answered us. The fault is always in the *way* we prayed — in the method or technique.

The mechanistic approach to prayer lends itself to abuse because it allows us to 'objectify' the problem. We can apportion blame when things do not work out as hoped, either by suggesting that the formula has not been followed correctly or that there is something wrong with the person praying. However, in such praying, the *system itself* is always immune from blame, and it is never assumed that God will do anything but respond to the correct form of prayer.

Because of this inherent 'protection' of a prayer formula, the mechanistic view of prayer for healing has to be seriously questioned.

EFFECTIVE HEALING PRAYER

There is another approach to healing prayer which is neither fatalistic, nor mechanistic. It is predicated on trust in a loving God, whose intervention in the lives of those who pray or are prayed for is related to their faith and expectation, but not dependent on them. This approach offers neither a guarantee of success, nor does it suggest that there is only one correct way to pray. Equally, it does not apportion blame when the hoped-for answer does not eventuate.

However, there are enough inexplicable healings which have resulted from it to suggest ways of praying which have proved to be helpful. It is an approach which gives equal consideration to the nature of God and the nature of humanity, and sees healing in terms of wholeness. It is based on a relationship of *trust* in a loving God who is interested in the *whole* life of those who relate to him.

❏ Healing prayer means believing that God is trustworthy

This approach to prayer for healing goes beyond the idea that it is good enough to focus prayer on any concept of God which is acceptable to the person praying, because the attitude of faith is more important than the One in whom that faith is placed. Instead, it relies on there being a sense of personal relationship between the person praying and the One to whom the prayers are directed. This relationship is generally understood in terms of the whole of life and does not depend on the outcome of prayer. It is a relationship of faith, based on trust in God.

For Christians, this relationship is particularly intimate because they believe that they are acceptable to God through forgiveness rather than through the prerequisite of good works or living an exemplary lifestyle. This demonstration of God's love for them encourages them to trust him not just with their ultimate destiny, but also with the details of their everyday life. They believe that they can trust God no matter what the circumstances of their lives because a fundamental tenet of the belief system is that *God is trustworthy*.

This gives them the courage to pray for healing. Prayer which is predicated on a basic trust in God is sometimes referred to as 'the prayer of faith'.

❑ Healing prayer means believing that God is able and willing to act

The prayer of faith does not just depend on a relationship of trust between those praying and the One to whom they are directing their prayers, but must also include a strong belief in the ability and willingness of that One to hear and answer prayer. Without this, there would be no point to prayer for healing.

It is in the interest of those who have faith in this sense to ensure that their faith is reinforced by whatever means they can. As this faith is basically an attitude, it can be reinforced by such traditional means as inspirational reading or acquaintance with stories of those who have had their prayers answered. It can also be reinforced by positive attitudes.

It is important when praying for healing that faith in the ability and willingness of God to answer prayer does not waver, but remains strong.

❑ Healing prayer means believing that God will act in our best interests

If prayer is approached with this trust in God and a strong belief in his ability and willingness to hear and answer prayer, there can be a high expectation that he will act towards the people praying or those being prayed for in a way that is best for them. This includes bringing miraculous healing of body, mind and spirit, resolving relationship difficulties or changing circumstances. When praying, the expectation is that healing will come, whether or not it is in the way that was first hoped.

*   *   *

The major components of healing prayer are, therefore, trust in a loving God, faith in his ability and willingness to hear and answer prayer, and a realistic expectation that he will hear our prayer and act in our best interests. Each of these components stems from a belief system which the individual is free to choose or reject.

However, unless the choice that is made includes all three components, prayer for healing is limited in some way and may lead to disappointment.

If trust in God is left out of the choice, healing prayer is limited to the mind-body connection, which leaves very little room for the supernatural.

If attitudes of the mind are left out, there is very little opportunity for the power of the mind to affect the healing process in a positive way.

A proper approach to prayer for healing must include the possibility of supernatural intervention as well as allowing the powerful mind-body connection to have its full effect.

However, having done all this, no guarantees can be offered that the healing outcome we desire will happen. It is all, ultimately, in God's hands.

4

When healing doesn't happen

THE STORY OF ROSEMARY'S HEALING is remarkable, though not unique. However, it leads us to the inevitable conclusion that sometimes the only explanation we can offer for an otherwise inexplicable healing is that of a miracle. When that miracle is as closely associated with prayer, as Rosemary's healing was, we are tempted to draw lessons from it which may be applicable to other situations.

We may be tempted to think that if enough people are praying and they have enough faith, then healing will automatically follow. Of course, this puts those who are *not* healed in similar circumstances in a difficult position. It implies either that they themselves did not have enough faith to be healed, or that they did not have enough friends to pray for them.

Both these suggestions are absurd, especially when we are looking beyond ourselves for healing to God who, by any definition, cannot be manipulated by our actions.

All we can say with any certainty in Rosemary's case, for instance, is that there was a lot of believing prayer by many people over a long period of time and that the healing took place. The reason God chose to heal Rosemary in this way will always remain a mystery, locked within the mind of God. We can only be thankful for it and for any other healings which take place by miraculous means. Moreover, we can be encouraged by such miracles to pray in faith for healing ourselves whenever we are faced with illnesses or problems of any sort, but we cannot devise a foolproof method of making it happen or offer any guarantees about the outcome of prayer.

When miracles of healing occur contrary to all medical expectation, it is always helpful to look at what was going on at the time and to learn from it. Otherwise, we are left wondering whether what happened was merely a chance occurrence. To think about healing only in terms of chance merely reinforces an attitude which is unproductive when it comes to healing. At its most positive, this attitude is one of acceptance of the present circumstances as inevitable. For some people, coming to the point of accepting present circumstances enables them to come to terms with their problem, but it does not necessarily give them any incentive to do anything about it.

There is no denying that it is often very important to work through a problem and to come to terms with it, especially if it has life-threatening or life-disturbing implications. However, if this process leads to fatalism rather than realism, it is not helpful in terms of healing.

At its most negative, to think about miraculous healing as a chance occurrence can result in a sense of hopelessness. Hopelessness is a feeling which often causes a person to give up on, or even give in to, their problem. Hopelessness nearly always works against healing. Believing prayer is neither a form of fatalism, nor an expression of hopelessness. It is a deliberate expression of faith in God and of dependence upon him in time of need.

In Rosemary's case, it is clear that she herself and those who were praying for her had faith and never gave up hope of a miracle. Their faith was based on their belief in a personal God to whom they felt they could entrust Rosemary in their prayers. Because of their faith, they did not feel that they had to accept the medical prognosis as inevitable. Nor did they consider it unrealistic to pray for a miracle.

Their prayer was not based on denial or self-delusion, but was rooted in a faith which enabled them to look beyond the present circumstances to a God whom they knew was capable of performing a miracle and whom they trusted, whether or not he performed that miracle. Experience had taught them that sometimes miracles occur which defy the medical prognosis and all reasonable expectation. They also understood the positive effect of faith on the healing process of the human body. Therefore, they prayed in faith for a miracle, but were prepared to leave the outcome to God.

All faith is based on a belief system. However, when faith becomes part of the way we pray for healing, it encompasses very important attitudes towards present circumstances and future hopes. It is this combination of faith and positive attitudes which seems to have such a powerful impact on the healing process.

Sceptics might suggest that this results in little more than wishful thinking on the part of those who pray. It is much more than this. Wishful thinking is something which is confined to the mind. Faith is always focussed beyond the self and believes for a miracle. Such faith is reinforced by positive attitudes, but is never replaced by them.

However, that does not mean that all those who pray or are prayed for in this way are always healed.

In my own work, I have sat with those in desperate need and felt powerless when no amount of prayer has made any difference to their condition. I have also watched a number of people die when there has seemed no reason for it: young people in the prime of life, stricken by a deadly disease in unfortunate circumstances; victims of accident for whom no amount of prayer or faith has had any effect; middle-aged men who have lost all interest in life, succumbing to illnesses for which there are known cures and good prognoses when treated effectively, but to whom no amount of love or counselling could restore any hope or meaning in life.

There seems to be a great mystery in all of this and it would be easy to say that it is simply not worth the effort involved in praying in faith for healing when the end result may well be disappointment. Nevertheless, the fact that some are healed is enough to encourage perseverance, even if it means living with some difficult questions, such as why some are healed and others are not.

GRAEME'S STORY OF DISAPPOINTMENT

Why Graeme was not healed will always be a mystery. It would be easy to say that his death was the result of contracting a deadly tropical disease while on holiday and leave it at that. However, the chance of contracting that particular disease was so small that when the vaccine sometimes recommended to those travelling in the region where he was going was not readily available, he didn't pursue the matter. Although the risk was negligible, Graeme caught the disease. The treatment proved to be ineffective and, two weeks later, he died.

There were a number of minor miracles along the way. The fact that he got back to Australia in the first place was a miracle in itself, because the symptoms of his disease only became evident after he had boarded his flight. Otherwise, he would not have been allowed to travel. However, the truth remains that the miracle everyone was praying for simply did not occur, even though there were many who thought it should. After all, Graeme was a man of faith, as were his family and friends. In their prayers, they were desperately believing that Graeme would be healed.

His parents and friends organised prayer meetings and less formal prayer took place virtually non-stop throughout his illness. Minor changes in his condition were reported which gave cause for hope. Graeme himself, however, was either delirious or unconscious during the entire time and in the end he died, despite the best medical attention available in the world and despite non-stop believing prayer.

Graeme's death, like all untimely deaths, was a tragedy. He was a young man who had much to contribute to society and the world at large through his professional expertise and personal qualities. In fact, one of the reasons for his trip overseas was to investigate the possibility of using his skills in the service of others by working in one of the needy developing countries of Asia. His death seemed to make no sense at all, especially from the perspective of faith in a loving God who cares for his own and who hears the prayers of those who believe in him.

THE PAIN OF DISAPPOINTMENT

Disappointment such as that surrounding Graeme's death and the failure of others to find healing is often very hard to come to terms with. This is particularly true for those who expect God to answer their prayers provided they pray in the correct way and for long enough. Graeme's death clearly demonstrates that prayer cannot be predicated on that particular basis.

We must never fall into the trap of thinking that God can somehow be controlled or manipulated by our actions. There is no formula for prayer which guarantees success. If there were, God would merely be a puppet on a string, even if we glorified that string by calling it faith. That would make God less powerful than ourselves and make nonsense of any meaningful concept of faith as part of the healing process.

If we take that viewpoint, we are no longer directing our prayers to the One who is more powerful than ourselves when we appeal to him for help, but are seeking to control or manipulate God by applying what we consider to be the correct formula. However, if God is all powerful and worthy of having our appeal for healing directed towards him, he cannot be manipulated in any way, not even by faith. Prayer and faith are the means of *asking* for God's help, not demanding it.

We will never know why praying in faith worked for Rosemary, but not for Graeme. After all, both were given little chance of survival and both were prayed for in very similar ways and just as fervently. Nevertheless, despite the ever-present risk of disappointment, those who were praying for Rosemary and Graeme felt that they had no alternative but to pray and believe for a miracle. The hope that a miracle might occur overrode the fear of disappointment and kept them going to the very end.

THE NATURE OF FAITH

If there can be no guarantees in regard to faith, then we have to ask why we should bother to pray for healing at all? The answer lies in the nature of faith itself.

Faith is generally qualified as being *in* something

or someone. In that sense, it is projected onto another, usually seen as external to the self and considered to have power in relation to the one who has the faith.

In a medical setting, for example, that power might be seen as residing in the doctor or in the medicine which has been prescribed — or even in the high-tech instruments and machines being used in the treatment. Patients believe in one or other or all of these for healing. In that sense, they are exercising faith.

Faith of this sort engenders a high expectation that healing will take place and is recognised as a powerful factor in the way patients respond to their treatment. For this reason, it is usually not discouraged by those responsible for the treatment, because it is beneficial to the patient's healing. Faith, even when focussed on medical procedures or on those carrying them out, always has a positive effect on the natural healing processes of the body. The reason for this can be found in the mind-body connection, which we will look at later.

Outside the medical setting, when faith is projected onto someone or something less easily identifiable, but also perceived as having power, the process is much the same and equally valid. There is the same high expectation of healing and the same positive effect on the way patients respond to their healing. Faith which is directed in this way is usually described as being in God and raises all sorts of possibilities beyond the parameters of medical prediction.

Such faith has many benefits. First, it leaves room for the unexpected and the inexplicable, in the form of a miracle. Second, it increases the possibility of accessing the power of the mind and utilising the powerful mind-body connection in the healing process in a context where these are recognised as ways in which God works in the lives of people. Third, it gives a great deal of incentive to get one's life in order, by dealing with unhealed emotions and broken relationships. Healing in these areas will unlock the natural healing processes of the body and make it easier to experience the positive intervention of God, whether through natural means or by a miracle.

This is why it is possible to have hope when everything seems hopeless and why faith sustains people to the very end. For even if the miracle does not occur, there are often many benefits to be gained along the way.

Faith when focussed on the known has limited expectations but, when focussed on the unknown, it has unlimited expectations. In the case of both Rosemary and Graeme, faith in the medical resource was very important, even though in the end it offered very little hope of recovery. Faith in God offered the only hope that remained. That hope was expressed in prayer by believing that God would stop the natural course of their illness and heal them. For Rosemary, that happened. For Graeme, however, it didn't.

Praying in faith to the God whose power is greater than ours opens up possibilities for healing which go beyond the known medical resource. Faith is a powerful attitude which not only affects the healing processes of the body in a positive way, but also offers the hope that the unexpected may happen and healing take place, contrary to all expectation. It depends on God to act favourably, but it offers no absolute guarantee of success in every situation.

However, because healing is a concept which includes the whole of life and not just the presenting problem, even when complete healing does not occur, there are often unexpected benefits. These benefits can often be directly attributed to the prayer and faith of the person praying or being prayed for and to their relationship with God. Therefore, they are outcomes of faith in the same way that complete healing would be and must be considered as healings in their own right. They might even be referred to correctly as miracles because they are the direct result of prayer and faith.

THE ABUSE OF FAITH

There are always those who refuse to accept the possibility of miracles, no matter how much evidence is presented to them. They usually justify their stance on rational grounds and prefer to rely on scientific medicine as the only means of healing available. They will generally have nothing to do with prayer for healing because they claim that it raises false expectations and often results in deep hurt when the hoped-for miracle does not eventuate.

Equally, there are those on the opposite extreme who link prayer and healing so closely together that they will not allow for the possibility of failure. Those who take this position have a real problem when healing does not occur. They explain the failure of healing as a lack of faith and tend to blame it either on those seeking the healing or those praying for them. This puts enormous pressure on those seeking healing through prayer either to deny the illness, or to act foolishly with regard to the treatment they are receiving.

I remember one young woman who was so inspired by a rousing call to believe that she would be healed and to demonstrate such a faith by throwing away all medication, that she did so, despite the risks involved and the attempts of those who knew her to talk her out of it. A few days later, she drowned in her bath while suffering a fit. Her death could have been avoided if she had remained on her medication. As if her death was not bad enough, I was appalled to hear the person who had issued the call to get rid of all medication as a sign of faith say, when told of her death, that she died because she did not have enough faith.

Such irresponsibility is unfortunately not uncommon, especially amongst practitioners of some alternative therapies. However, it represents a complete misunderstanding of the nature of faith and usually causes more harm than healing.

The motive in issuing a call to faith such as this may be well-intentioned. It may be an attempt to encourage people to focus their whole attention on what they are hoping for as a result of prayer and not to be sidetracked by negative thoughts.

While it is important to be single-minded and positive when praying for healing, these attitudes can lead to reckless behaviour unless they are developed in a balanced way. They can contribute to denial about the seriousness of the problem being faced and even result in unnecessary harm or death. There is a delicate balance between faith and reality which must always be maintained when praying for healing. Because of this, caution and wisdom must be employed when encouraging those in need to believe for a miracle.

5

When healing comes with death

HEALING IS NOT ALWAYS BLACK AND WHITE. Healing is not just about whether a person is cured of their illness or not, but also about what happens during the process. If we accept the broad definition given earlier of healing as relating to the whole person — body, mind and spirit — it is possible to see healing as a process.

This process may include finding peace with God, peace with self, peace with others or peace with the world without necessarily being cured. For instance, I have known many people for whom the process of dying has brought much more healing to their lives than they ever thought possible. Their faith in God gave them much more than the physical cure they were hoping for.

Some found a measure of wholeness which

eluded them throughout their lives.

Death is often seen as failure, both by those who seek healing through prayer and in medicine. Those who pray for healing often see death as failure because God has not intervened to bring about a miracle. In medicine, death is sometimes seen as failure because science has been unable to triumph over nature. In both cases, death can result in a sense of guilt or even recrimination as a result of this feeling of failure.

However, it may be more helpful to see death as a natural part of life. This way of looking at death enables us to avail ourselves of all the resources available to combat it in the physical, emotional and spiritual realms, while taking whatever opportunities the process of dying offers for healing in the broadest sense of the word. Most people when faced with a terminal illness seem to say that they are not so much afraid of death as of dying. However contradictory it may seem, it is possible to transform the process of dying into a healing experience.

I have already mentioned the way in which the threat of imminent death enabled one person I know to deal with a distressing broken relationship and, as a result, experience physical healing. Many others have shared similar experiences over the years.

To illustrate the healing effect of imminent death, I would like to refer to three men I knew well. They

all died prematurely of cancer even though they
were prayed for in faith. One was a young man, one
a middle-aged man, and one a little older. Each
found a measure of healing in death by being at peace
with God, at peace within, at peace with others, or
at peace with the world.

The young man's story is quite distinctive. The
other two had much in common. Both died of
cancer after living with it for more than twenty
years. However, they were both very different
people in terms of their background, experience of
life, attitudes, understanding of faith and the way
they faced death.

THE STORY OF RICHARD'S DEATH

The story of Richard's death began a few months
before his parents brought him to the residential
healing home where I was working at the time. He
had just been diagnosed as having cancer. It had
spread rapidly and he was not expected to live more
than a couple of months at the most. He was only
seventeen and, until recently, a very active and
rebellious teenager. There was no cure for his cancer
and the only medical resource available was palliative care and pain management.

Understandably, he was very angry at the way
life had turned out for him. Richard's anger was
directed at God or anyone he saw as a God substitute,

including his doctors, his counsellors and especially me.

Although he only planned to stay with us a few days, it took some time to build any sort of relationship with him. His parents despaired. They had come in the hope that, through prayer, something might be done for their son. There was literally no other hope for him. Being realistic about his prognosis, they were as concerned about his emotional and spiritual well-being as for his physical condition. Nevertheless, they never gave up hoping for a miracle.

While Richard was with us, two unexpected things happened. A desperately ill, two-year-old baby boy died suddenly in his mother's arms and a gentle, seventy-five-year-old woman, Evelyn, found peace with God and came to terms with the inevitability of her own imminent death from cancer of the throat. Both unrelated events were to have a healing impact upon Richard's life.

When the little boy died, Richard fell apart. He became hysterical and self-destructive. Nobody could get near him, not even the doctor called to administer the medication which might have helped. Nobody except Evelyn. She and Richard had formed a close friendship. They had a common bond. Because they were both dying, they were able to talk to each other about death in a way that they could not talk to anyone else. Evelyn had come to terms with death, though Richard at that time had not.

The baby's death acted as a catalyst, unlocking all the anger, pain and grief that Richard was experiencing about his own coming death. Evelyn was able to go to him on the basis of their friendship and let him off-load it all. She did a superb job of listening to Richard and encouraging him. During the time they spent together, Richard was able to come to terms enough with what was happening to him to turn for help in dealing with the spiritual and emotional turmoil he was experiencing. There's nothing particularly unusual in this except that he did so by discovering faith.

It was Evelyn who, because of the suffering and prospect of death which they had in common, was able to help Richard discover for himself the same faith that she had. On the basis of that faith, he found peace with the God with whom he had previously been so angry and eventually, with the help of some counselling and prayer, he found peace within himself.

He left us a few days later and died within a month. His parents wrote and told us how he had died at peace because of the healing he had received spiritually and emotionally while with us.

They also told us of a dream he had the night he

died. In the dream, he was aware of himself standing apart, watching a crowd of ghost-like figures who had their backs to him and were moving away from him at the time, wailing in fear. He felt very lonely and afraid.

Then, out of the crowd came Evelyn, smiling and stretching out her hand to him and inviting him to come with her to another place. At that moment, all his fear left him and he happily went with her. The anguished cries which had accompanied the first part of this dream had woken his parents who came into his room. As they comforted him, he recounted the dream to them. When he had finished, he died peacefully in their arms, a smile upon his face.

What neither he nor his parents knew at the time was that Evelyn had died the night before. No particular emphasis can be placed on this coincidence. It was just a dream. And yet it illustrates the difference that being at peace with God can make in dying. In Richard's case, that peace came through the friendship of a gracious, older woman whose faith had sustained her throughout her life and gave her courage and hope in death. Her faith and friendship, combined with the prayer and counselling Richard received, changed his death from a terrifying experience to one of healing and growth.

Richard came to terms with death and died at

peace because of his new-found faith and the friendship of someone who shared it — and his suffering — with him.

THE STORY OF HARRY'S DEATH

Harry was in his middle years when he died of cancer. Twice in recent years I had been made aware, with some distress, of a recurrence in the cancer for which Harry had been successfully treated almost twenty years previously. The treatment was successful on the first of these two occasions and the prognosis looked good.

However, when the cancer flared up again and began to spread quite rampantly a second time, things looked much more grim. In fact, his medical advisers began to suggest that, although they would have expected him in the normal course of events to live for a number of years with the disease, in fact he would probably not survive many months.

In the end, his death came even more quickly than that. After receiving the prognosis, he decided that he had had enough and opted for no further medical intervention, apart from what was necessary to make him comfortable and relatively free of pain. He died very soon after that.

I had had a reasonably close professional relationship with Harry over the years, so it was only natural that I should spend some time with him towards the end of his life. As I did so, I noticed that many of the deep emotional traumas of the past, particularly his childhood, remained with him and were still largely unresolved.

I and many others had listened for years to him recount the effects on his life of a childhood disrupted by the trauma of wartime England. This was further complicated by a feeling of rejection by his parents when they sent him to boarding school at a very young age and the lack of any demonstrative expression of emotion in his upbringing. He often spoke of his early years in boarding school as being full of fear and loneliness. The frequent beatings and caning he received, usually without explanation, left him with a deeply ingrained lack of trust in relationships and a defensive shell from which he rarely felt secure enough to emerge. He always felt socially inadequate.

There were happy times and good memories of course and, although he felt no bitterness towards his parents for the way they had treated him as a child and developing adolescent, he always had a sense of loss about his childhood. This robbed him of any real enjoyment of life in later years.

After leaving school, he joined the Royal Air Force, underwent officer training, and experienced something of the security and acceptance which he had missed out on during his earlier years. The positive experience of his military service, his subsequent marriage and family life in Australia and a challenging new career went a long way towards balancing the trauma of his childhood and adolescence. However, it was not enough to enable him to break free from the past and the emotional limitations it had imposed upon him. In some ways, he saw death as an escape from the emptiness of his life.

Harry was a believer and had undergone extensive counselling in his later years. However, nothing seemed to change the way he felt about himself. Most people would have thought of him as reserved. They would have neither guessed the extent of the fears and doubts he lived with, nor the effect they had on his inner life.

The miracle of Harry's death was that it enabled him to break out of his defensive shell. For one brief time in his life, he was able to reach out to those who were closest to him and heal many of the misunderstandings and hurts which had occurred over the years. This was not an easy process. It took a lot of personal courage and help from God which those closest to him are convinced came as a result of prayer.

It is certainly true that the courage to deal with the unfinished business of his life came from Harry's faith in God. He knew that it would only be with God's help that he would be able to act out of character by stepping out of his protective shell and revealing something of his hidden self to others. He also knew that, once that step of faith was taken, it would only be with God's continued help that he would find the courage to heal the relationships that were important to him.

That courage didn't come easily to a man who had built such strong defences around his emotions. In the end, it came as the result of a number of coincidences. A succession of people who knew Harry, but knew little about the inner workings of his being, visited him and in their conversations with him made comments and suggestions which proved to be incredibly significant to him, even though they were completely unaware of it themselves.

It was as if these coincidences had been deliberately planned to challenge Harry and make it difficult for him not to act on them. They seemed too deliberate not to have a purpose behind them. It appeared both to Harry and to those who were praying for him that God was using the circumstances of his death to bring healing to him.

Harry was aware that he always had the choice whether or not to act but, because of what was happening, he saw that God was giving him the opportunity of facing up to the issues in his life which were troubling him and of finding peace within himself and healing for some of his damaged relationships.

I have seen this sort of thing happen many times. The power of God at work in the lives of those who believe in him often matches their need in a way that is right for them at the time, even if others would like the outcome to be different.

There are innumerable ways in which this can work out. However, one striking feature of it is the way in which the integrity of the person involved is always respected by God and the choice whether or not to take the opportunity offered them to find healing is always left up to them.

Harry wasn't healed physically and he didn't completely lose his fear or loneliness. However, the healing of relationships which he experienced towards the end of his life was beyond his wildest expectation when he was well. He died, having tied up many of the loose ends of his life. This could only be good for those who were left behind as they sought to make sense of his death and learn to live without him. It certainly made it easier for Harry to die at peace.

Faith enabled Harry to find the courage to deal with the unfinished business of his life and to recognise that God was able to make dying a healing experience for him and for those he loved so dearly. He was supported by many members of his family and friends who were praying in faith that God would bring healing to Harry at the end of his life. Their prayers were answered in a remarkable way.

THE STORY OF KEN'S DEATH

Ken was not just a friend, but a colleague. Like Harry, he had had cancer for a number of years and had learnt to live with it. However, unlike Harry, his form of cancer was usually much faster in spreading and, from the very beginning, his medical prognosis was not good. In fact, he defied all expectation when the cancer went into long-term remission.

When eventually it flared up again and required surgery, Ken took the unusual step of informing only a handful of friends and colleagues whom he knew to be people of faith and whom he trusted to pray positively for him to be healed. It was very important for him to know that he was upheld only by positive thoughts and prayer, for he considered that negative thoughts when translated into negative prayer were counterproductive to healing. Ken had learnt this lesson through many years of involvement in praying for others.

Having shared his need for healing with those whom he trusted to pray positively and to speak words of faith to him, Ken was confident that healing would come. He did not neglect the medical resource, but made equally sure that the surgeon he chose had the same positive outlook that he did. Again, he defied the odds by not only recovering fully from the operation and subsequent therapy, but by going into long-term remission once again.

It was a number of years before the cancer returned and finally claimed his life. In the meantime, he had lived a very full and active life. Not only was he working more than full-time despite being well beyond the usual retirement age, but he was also involved in helping others right up to the time of his final illness. Life was very satisfying for him and he shared it fully with his wife. Ken considered his positive outlook to be an outworking of his faith and he never differentiated between the two things. It was both his faith and attitude which more than anything else dominated his approach to life and enabled him to face its many trials.

Despite this approach, things weren't always easy for Ken. His early life was not ideal, but it did have a certain amount of stability in it. This stood him in good stead for some of the things he experienced later on.

He joined the army at a very young age during World War II and experienced some of the horrors of war. He married young, had a wonderfully supportive wife, raised a family and was involved in various business ventures throughout his working life. Like so many others, he knew both success and failure in business, his positive attitude being important in both.

As a committed Christian from early boyhood, his beliefs always played an important part in his life and gave him confidence. He dared to have such an outlook in life because of his faith in God. He put this positive faith to good use through his involvement in a number of innovative ventures in various churches, all of which are still flourishing. He was also actively involved in praying for people to be healed.

Despite all of this, Ken experienced a number of setbacks in life. At times, he had to face the hostility of those jealous of his successes and even suffered the pain of alienation from members of his own family for a time. There were many disappointments with people in business and in the church. Yet nothing ever swayed him from his positive attitude. Therefore, it surprised me a little when, during his last illness, he began to acknowledge that death may be imminent.

The surprise I felt was not related to the acceptance of death, because as long as I had known Ken he had always been realistic about sickness and death, while at the same time maintaining his positive outlook. There was never any suggestion in Ken's mind of a contradiction between realism and positivism. The one was always predicated on the other.

My surprise was that he saw his imminent death as a positive, God-given opportunity to get his house in order. He never accepted any suggestions the doctors made about how long he might have to live, because he considered such talk as negative. He believed that God would give him enough time to deal with a number of unresolved issues within his family, to heal some difficult relationships and to grow spiritually through the experience.

While never giving up hope that another miracle of healing might occur in his life as had happened in the past, he approached the matters he needed to deal with in the same way that he approached everything in life. He prayed that God would give him the opportunities he needed and the right words to say. As a result, some of those opportunities came in unusual ways, even through the tragic death of someone he loved very deeply.

By the time he died, he had the joy of having all his prayers in this regard answered. He died in the same way that he had lived — full of faith, positive to the very end and actively concerned to put things right with others, as much for their sake as for his own.

Ken's dying, like his living, was a positive experience, despite all the horrors of the disease from which he suffered. Healing for him included both the miracles he had experienced through the long course of his cancer as a result of both prayer and the medical treatment he received, and the opportunity of being at peace with God, with himself and with others at the end of his life.

The attitude that was so much part of his faith enabled him not just to live well, but also to die well. This was a wonderful end to a life of positive faith.

HEALING THROUGH DEATH

The fundamental truth we learn from these three stories is that, even in death, healing can occur. The faith and attitudes we develop in life and the opportunities we have taken for spiritual growth and emotional healing can affect not only the course of an illness, but also the way in which we approach death and dying. And, as Richard's story shows, it is never too late to begin.

Ken's positive approach to life, to combating illness and to facing death — coupled with his faith in God — enabled him to make the most of every opportunity he had and to grow through it. He approached his death in the same way that he lived life and found a remarkable amount of healing and growth through the process of dying.

Harry, on the other hand, because of the experiences he had in childhood and adolescence, tended to have a more negative outlook. Consequently, he failed to find any real fulfilment in life despite all the blessings which came his way. It was only with the help of many people towards the end of his life that he was able develop a change of attitude towards himself and towards life in general. This, in turn, helped him deal with some of the issues which had troubled him for so long and brought a measure of healing of relationships at the very end of his life.

The negativity, which characterised his life as a result of the experiences he had in his early life, affected his faith, his health and his relationships adversely. It had a huge impact on the way he lived and died and it was so deeply ingrained that he never actually managed to resolve it, even though he was able to transcend it, at least in part, in the final weeks of his life.

Richard discovered that peace with God enabled him to cope with his anger at dying and face death with hope for the future. Richard's peace came through faith in God through Christ. It was the friendship of another sufferer who brought him to faith and enabled him to die well.

If we can learn anything from these three stories, it is that faith doesn't always bring healing. However, the sort of faith we have and the attitudes which accompany it will affect every aspect of our life and even determine the way we die. In this sense, there can be healing — even in death.

6

How mind and body work together in healing I

IT IS CLEAR FROM THE STORIES of Richard, Harry and Ken that emotions and attitudes play an important part in the way people face death. The same is true about the way people deal with any form of accident, disease, sickness or general disruption to their lives. The primary concern of those facing such situations is always the hope of a cure or a change of circumstances.

Increasingly, however, the importance of having a different perspective on illness is being emphasised, especially when a cure seems unlikely. Many mainstream and alternative programs are being used by those who are suffering chronic pain, or facing the prospect of long-term disability or death, to try and harness the power of the mind in order to cope with their problems. There are many recognised benefits in these programs which contribute to a greater sense of well-being than would otherwise be possible.

Some of these programs have been devised and run in medical settings, some are self-help programs and others have been put together by alternative healing groups. A few of these offer extreme and somewhat simplistic answers to complex, life-threatening illnesses. However, without disparaging any of them, it is clear that the mind-body connection is now being taken seriously in both the cause and treatment of illness and is the subject of a great deal of experimentation, testing, evaluation and application in a wide range of medical settings.

There is a subtle shift in all of this from a *curative* approach, which concentrates on trying to effect a cure in all situations, to a *lifestyle* one, which seeks both to prevent the onslaught of illness and to enable those who are already suffering live longer and better. The healing process is moving beyond the limitations of looking for a cure to a concept of wholeness. It is no longer confined in theory or practice to whether or not a cure eventuates, but is just as concerned with quality of life.

As helpful as this is, we need to be wary lest this shift in approach leads us to fall into the trap of a lot of New Age thinking that all sickness is self-inflicted. Even when seeking to help a person find peace by dealing with unresolved hurts, repressed experiences, broken relationships or guilt over wrong-doing, it is important to avoid the conclusion that all sickness is the result of such activity.

Sometimes, of course, it may be. However, the assumption of self-inflicted illness epitomised by the catchcry 'I gave myself cancer' as a prelude to over-coming a particular illness or problem more often than not leads to guilt when the healing does not eventuate. It can also make the person vulnerable to spiritual and emotional exploitation. Genuine interest in the mind-body connection in sickness and healing is motivated by a desire to see people at peace or made whole, despite the final outcome.

Nevertheless, the mind-body connection is an important one. It needs to be understood for the part it plays in the healing process and dealt with when appropriate.

EILEEN'S STORY OF MIND-BODY HEALING

Eileen was a devoutly religious person in her mid-fifties who always asked for prayer for physical healing on a particular day each year. Her need for healing was very real. She had a life-threatening, congenital liver complaint which left her incapable of living independently or functioning in the role expected of her in a large girls' school.

In fact, to all intents and purposes, she had been

an invalid for twelve years. As she was a nun, she could not easily withdraw without creating difficulties for the small order to which she belonged. She struggled on, mostly engaged in administration, but effectively only able to do the job for about one-third of the time. She was seriously ill, had a poor medical prognosis and no medical solution to rely on. Her condition had been getting worse over the past year and she was quite desperate.

It was probably her rapidly declining condition which made her break her usual habit of not talking about herself when asking for prayer. This time she decided to ask for some counselling as preparation for prayer. Apart from her physical condition, she was feeling guilty about letting the side down and was troubled by some old thoughts that kept recurring. What she wanted was to be at peace with God so that she could pray for a miracle, as the medication she was on seemed to be losing its effectiveness.

When we met for counselling, it became clear that her emotional needs were as pressing as her physical ones. It appears that she harboured a deep resentment towards her parents for the way they treated her as a teenager and she still felt the sting of a bitter disappointment resulting from a failed romance in her early twenties. Her disappointment had been compounded by the sense of failure she felt at not being able to meet the obligations of her religious life. It was further complicated by recent contact with her former fiancé, who was now the priest responsible for saying mass at the convent where she lived.

As we talked, the unresolved feelings she had about the past very quickly rose to the surface. Over a number of sessions, she was able to deal with her resentment, bitterness, anger, guilt and the sense of unworthiness she carried deep within her much more quickly than I thought would be possible.

Prayer played a large part in these sessions, especially prayers of forgiveness which were deeply significant, given her background, and proved to be very therapeutic. We prayed for peace within herself, peace in her relationship with her former fiancé which was now very different to what it had been in the past, and peace with God. The sessions were not easy because her condition was so bad that she had to lie flat on the floor during them. She had to be driven home immediately after them because of the pain she was experiencing.

When the day she had appointed for prayer for physical healing arrived, she felt well-prepared and was visibly at peace. She surprised us all by deciding to sit for the prayer rather than continue to lie on the floor, where she had been up to that point. After we finished praying, I noticed that she continued sitting rather than returning to the floor as we would have expected. I had never seen her sit for any length of time before, so I was amazed to see her remain seated for some time after the prayer had finished and stay behind to socialise with those who had prayed for her. We would normally have expected her to be driven home immediately because of the pain. Something significant had obviously happened.

In fact, Eileen had been healed physically in an unostentatious but lasting way. Nothing dramatic took place apart from some simple prayers and the laying-on of hands. The only feature of any note about the whole episode was the period of preparation. It occurred when other unhealed areas of her life were dealt with and thus she expected that healing would take place. She was unswerving in her faith on this point.

I can only surmise from this that for Eileen, the mind-body connection was very strong. This meant that the feelings she had suppressed for more than thirty years were so interconnected with her physical condition that her body had not responded to medical treatment or healing prayer. This could only happen when the emotions which had had such a debilitating effect on her physical and emotional well-being had been resolved.

As a result of this healing, Eileen was able to return to full-time work, choosing not to go back to education, but to take up the more demanding role of pastoral assistant in a nearby parish. She now has a new lease on life and enjoys a very satisfying lifestyle. It is hard to imagine that she had been so ill.

It has been said that a calm mind is the key to good health. That is a shorthand way of describing the role the emotions play in healing, especially given the importance of the mind-body connection. There can be no doubt, for instance, that negative attitudes can counteract the effects of positive faith and can have a disastrous effect on medical treatment.

Harry's story, which is referred to in the previous chapter, is a good illustration of the way in which negative attitudes can affect a person's state of well-being and rob them of wholeness. Eileen's story highlights the role that emotions can play in determining a person's sense of well-being and even in preventing physical healing.

It is possible that, in some circumstances, emotions may cause physical illness — though again I would caution against making this connection in every case.

THE ROLE OF POSITIVE THINKING IN HEALING
Attitudes such as positive thinking have long been recognised as affecting a person's well-being and

approach to life. Books have been written about it and motivational training programs devised around it.

For instance, I once had a neighbour who was the living embodiment of this type of teaching and a successful salesman because of it. He used to wake up early every morning, leap out of bed, throw open the window and shout 'Hello world! What a beautiful day' — no matter what the weather. He claimed that it set him in the right frame of mind for the rest of the day by making him feel positive. With that mindset, he believed that he could overcome any difficulty he might face during the day.

And it seemed to work for him. He started each day by reinforcing his positive attitudes in order to get through the day.

This is not all that far removed from those who use prayer and meditation to reinforce their faith in God and to face each day with renewed strength and confidence. Their belief in God becomes the basis on which they build a positive attitude, which allows them to look beyond themselves for help in facing each day and even allows them to hope for the unexpected, if their circumstances warrant it.

Whether we're talking about positive thinking or the limited understanding of faith just mentioned, both are attitudes which affect our well-being and, as such, are part of the growing interest in the mind-body connection and its relation to healing. Both utilise the mind, though in different ways. Positive thinking finds the source of healing within and seeks to harness the power of the mind to overcome sickness. This mind over matter approach often centres around the idea that the power to heal lies within and that the release of that power depends on having the right attitude to the problem and to healing.

Faith, on the other hand, looks outwards for the source of healing and tends to rely on God to bring it about. Both these approaches are considered to be helpful in promoting healing and are finding increased support in medical circles. They are at present the subject of a great deal of research and long-term psychological studies, the results of which are beginning to be made available to the general reader as well as the specialist.

Those who pray in faith for healing have always recognised the importance of attitudes and the effect they have on the healing process. However, distinctions need to be drawn between the power of positive thinking and faith. The two should not be confused, even though faith incorporates positive attitudes when applied to healing.

Faith not only includes the positive attitudes which facilitate healing, but has a spiritual dimension to it. For it looks beyond the inner resources of attitude and mind to the One whose power is greater and whom we can trust with our problem. This not only impacts positively on the healing process, but also accepts the possibility of miracles occurring.

This interaction between faith in God and positive attitudes often result in miraculous healing — as the following story illustrates.

7

How mind and body work together in healing II

HOPELESSNESS, HELPLESSNESS, ALONENESS (or abandonment) and worthlessness are powerful emotions which can be destructive if they are not resolved. These deep-seated emotions are usually masked by others such as anger, hatred, bitterness, resentment and rejection. This being the case, it often takes a great deal of expertise to work through the different emotional layers to get to the primary emotions which may be affecting a person's state of well-being.

There are differing views about the importance of this task for healing and there are many different techniques for achieving it. However, without entering into that particular debate, it needs to be said that there are times when a person's state of well-being can be greatly affected by their emotions and that such occasions cannot be ignored if healing is to take place. Moreover, healing can be inhibited, or even prevented, by unresolved emotional hurts — and there is good evidence to suggest that in some instances physical problems may even have been caused by them. These reasons alone indicate the need to consider the emotions in the healing process and seek to do something about them if necessary.

Almost every story of healing mentioned in this book has an emotional component to it. Even those whose healing comes as the direct result of miraculous intervention usually find that this is only the beginning and that the miracle itself often leads to further healing of an emotional or spiritual kind. This reinforces what I have been saying about healing being related to the whole person, where change in one area of life is likely to have an effect on other areas as well. If that change is good, then the benefit will flow into the whole person and not be confined only to the area that originally needed healing.

The rapid growth in the popularity of courses in self-awareness, personal growth, relationship training and stress management in recent years is much more than a reflection of the emphasis on individual needs which has come into prominence over the past few decades. It illustrates a greater awareness in the general population of the importance of the emotions in attaining a state of well-being and a greater willingness on the part of health professionals to deal with the emotions in their attempts to prevent and treat illness.

It is no longer unusual to find counselling and group therapy prescribed alongside surgery and various forms of medically orientated therapy in the treatment of cancer or other diseases. These different ways of treating the whole person are no longer seen as competing with each other, but are considered to be complementary. Various support groups for a wide range of illnesses have developed as a result of this shift in emphasis and we even find the use of active listening and touch are now highly recommended and practised amongst the mainstream healing professions.

A friend of mine who has developed an illness which has implications for his quality of life and has significantly affected his lifestyle was recently invited by his specialist to attend the inaugural meeting of a support group for those suffering from this particular illness. The support group was being established and run by medical specialists and, to his surprise, apart from the expected lectures and advice on the latest techniques of managing the illness, speaker after speaker emphasised the importance of a healthy emotional life and positive attitudes as the key to delaying the progression of the illness and minimising its effects.

While they could not offer any cure, they stressed the importance of the mind-body connection and suggested ways of dealing with the emotions and building positive attitudes which would help in the management of this particular illness and life in general.

PENNY'S STORY OF MIND-BODY HEALING

Penny and her husband were well aware of the importance of resolving emotional hurts as both were involved in the caring professions. Penny had multiple sclerosis and eventually had to withdraw from her involvement in helping others when her illness became so bad that it made it almost impossible for her to get around. She had two young, dependent children and she was well aware that there was virtually no hope of a cure.

Penny and her husband felt desperate about the situation and asked if they could come and talk about it with a view to having prayer for healing. Penny was only just able to move with the aid of two walking sticks when they arrived. After I had spent some time with them together, Penny asked to see me alone.

It emerged from the conversations which followed over a period of time that there was a tension in her relationship with her husband and that they were not able to talk about it. This underlying tension in their marriage dated from the birth of her first child, who was microcephalic.

Penny felt enormous guilt because of his condition which she related to the circumstances surrounding his birth. At the time, Penny had been anxious to have children as soon as possible, but her husband had not been keen — partly because they were newly married and he felt they needed time to establish their relationship, though mainly because she was working in the radiotherapy section of the local hospital. The director of the department had felt it necessary to warn staff about the slight risk of birth defect if they worked there while pregnant. Against her husband's wishes and ignoring the warning that had been given, she had fallen pregnant and had continued working where she was.

Whether or not there had been any link between her work and her son's abnormality is difficult to determine. However, she blamed herself for it and in fact had never forgiven herself. This created the tension she felt in her relationship with her husband. She felt guilty because of what she had done and, because of her guilt, she felt unable to talk to him about it. She saw her son's condition as a punishment for her guilt.

Two years after the birth of her son, she told me, the first signs of multiple sclerosis began to appear and progressed fairly rapidly. As soon as possible after her disease was diagnosed, she and her husband had a second child, another boy, while they felt they could. The second child was perfectly normal, but the joy of his birth only served to compound her guilt.

As we explored this guilt which Penny felt, a deeper feeling of rejection linked to a sense of unworthiness and helplessness began to emerge. I began to suspect that these feelings might somehow explain the extent of the guilt she felt over the birth of her son. From what she said, it appeared that her father had walked out on her mother after a bitter and abusive marriage. As a little child, Penny felt that she was to blame for what happened between her mother and father.

In her own way, she had tried to do what she could to hold her parents' marriage together but, when she failed, she felt helpless. She perceived her father's leaving the marriage as a rejection of her, which in turn made her feel unloved and worthless. These feelings were reinforced by some experiences she had at school. She attended a selective school in a middle-class area and was made to feel different to the other girls because her parents were divorced. This was a real problem at the time she was growing up and at the school she attended, where most children came from stable homes.

Penny was a woman of strong faith and so, when

118/How mind and body work together in healing II

these things began to emerge, it was possible to encourage her to look to God for forgiveness in the areas of her perceived guilt and for the help she needed in resolving some of her unresolved emotions from childhood. It took time, but eventually she found peace within herself and was able to deal with the tensions in her relationship with her husband. Even though we had been praying for physical healing during the time we were able to talk together, it was only when she felt at ease with herself because of the forgiveness she had experienced from God and because of the emotional healing that had taken place that she was able to heal her relationship with her husband and to dare ask God for a miracle.

I am pleased to report that a miracle occurred.

Those of us who had gathered to pray for her were delighted when, after we had prayed, she stood up, handed us her walking sticks and walked out of the room unaided to get a cup of tea. The prayer session had not been long or distinctive in any way. Those who were there had certainly been praying for Penny for a long time and had faith enough in God to believe for a miracle. However, apart from their commitment and faith, the only remarkable thing about the gathering was Penny's healing itself.

The healing proved to be permanent. In fact, not long after it took place, she went off on a holiday with her family and sent me a photograph of her, her husband and two young sons happily enjoying long walks together in the mountains. She has been leading a normal life ever since.

In Penny's case, indeed, the mind-body connection was very strong and appears to have been linked to her illness in some way. The trauma of her son's birth defect and her guilt were important factors in her healing, as were the emotional damage of her childhood and adolescence. I doubt very much whether she would have found physical healing if she had not experienced emotional healing first.

However, as in the case of Eileen in the last chapter, we cannot draw any general conclusions about this in relation to multiple sclerosis or any other illness, except to highlight the importance of the mind-body connection for healing, whether in the medical setting or through prayer. No assumptions about the mind-body connection can be made in particular cases until it has been thoroughly tested. That can only be done with the permission of the person involved and only if it seems like the appropriate course of action to take.

THE ROLE OF EMOTIONAL TRAUMA IN ILLNESS

I recently met a woman who told me about an unusual series of accidents and illnesses she had experienced over the previous few years. Less than a year before I met her, she had been diagnosed with breast cancer which was so advanced that she had to undergo surgery and radiotherapy almost immediately.

She was totally confused by this string of what she called bad luck, particularly the cancer. Therefore, she was surprised when the doctor taking her medical history asked her a series of questions, some of which she expected, some she didn't. He wanted to know whether there was any history of cancer in her family or whether she had ever smoked. She replied in the negative.

However, when he asked whether there had been any recent trauma in her life, she could only reply that there certainly had. Two years before the cancer was discovered, her husband, to whom she was devoted and with whom she had spent a long and happy life, died unexpectedly. His death had been the beginning of the series of accidents and physical illnesses she mentioned, despite a healthy, accident-free life up until that time.

Her doctor seemed to think that the trauma of her husband's sudden death and the unresolved grief associated with it had somehow been instrumental in causing the cancer and suggested personal counselling along with the radical medical treatment which was necessary. Unfortunately, being a very private person and unused to sharing her feelings with anyone except her husband, she felt unable to take up the suggestion. At the time I met her, she was about to undergo a second bout of surgery and her prognosis looked very poor indeed.

I have always found the connection between emotional trauma and illness to be very real. I nearly always ask people who ask for prayer for healing if any major trauma or event has taken place in their lives up to two years or so before they developed their illness or the problem they are experiencing. In response, they often reveal some significant event which has impacted negatively upon them and remains unresolved. If this is the case, it is nearly always important to deal with it as part of their healing.

It is interesting to note, also, that this is becoming an orthodox position in some medical circles. Many doctors will now investigate whether there has been some emotional trauma prior to the development of an illness which could possibly be related to it. If such a link is discovered, it is usually dealt with either in personal or group therapy as part of the treatment being offered. It cannot be overlooked when praying for people to be healed.

The slogan 'stress is a killer' is an over-generalisation, although it does contain an element of truth. We know that there is good stress and bad stress and that a certain amount of stress is not a bad thing.

However, there is a level of stress which is recognised as dangerous to health. In some cases, it can contribute to hypertension and heart disease; there are those who think that it, along with other lifestyle factors, may be a cause of cancer. It is known to be a significant factor in other illnesses as well, some of which may well be a physical outworking of internal pressures or stress. Numerous studies have shown the link between stress at work and minor ailments and emotional disorders, and there is an increasing tendency to suspect that it plays a larger part in many disabling conditions.

Stress can be the result of external or internal pressure — or a combination of both. When the pressure is external, it is relatively easy to identify and deal with, even though it requires an active decision on the part of the sufferer to do so and a commitment to carry it through.

Internal pressure is usually linked to the emotions and is not always easy to identify or resolve. A good example of this is the businessman who is labelled a workaholic. He may, for instance, be subjecting himself to enormous demands at work because of relationship difficulties at home or because he is driven by a strong desire for the acceptance and approval he missed out on while growing up.

We all crave acceptance and approval but, when

it results in inappropriate and self-destructive behaviour, it may be that it is fed by an unresolved emotional need. The strong desire for acceptance and approval may be the result of unmet love by a parent who was perceived as being distant or unaccepting, a deep-seated feeling of unworthiness or any number of unresolved feelings. Stress can be caused by such unmet inner needs and the resulting anxiety, or by the unwillingness to say 'No' to external pressures which may be health-threatening because they represent the possibility of meeting an inner need.

If there is such a combination of pressures going on in a person's life, then stress can indeed be a killer. Most stress management courses recognise this and try to expose the underlying cause of the stress through the use of simple self-awareness exercises. In order to deal with it, they may suggest lifestyle changes, relationship training or personal counselling.

The only point I want to make here is that stress can be a major cause of illness and it needs to be considered seriously in the healing process, because it can involve physical, emotional, spiritual and lifestyle issues which affect a person's sense of well-being and wholeness. When praying for someone suffering stress to be healed, it may be necessary to pray for whatever is causing the stress. That may not be the obvious thing, but may lie in the emotions or relationships.

I have only touched on some of the obvious areas of the mind-body connection which are important in healing in the last two chapters. It has already been explored extensively and applied in medical settings to good effect. However, the whole area of the mind-body connection and the way in which faith affects it has an enormous contribution to make as some of the illustrations I have given show. Faith plays an important part in confronting and dealing with destructive attitudes, unresolved emotions and harmful lifestyles. When praying for healing, it is important to be aware of the mind-body connection and to pray appropriately.

In most settings, the focus is on the mind and the way in which it controls behaviour and affects treatment. The mind is also the centre of understanding, so the attitudes which people have towards their illness or problem will affect the cause of it. Similarly, the attitudes they have towards their healing will affect that process significantly. There are scientifically measurable ways of verifying this in relation to the natural healing agents in the body itself.

It is beyond doubt that we have to take the mind-body connection seriously.

8

How individual prayer can be part of the healing process

THERE ARE, AS WE HAVE SEEN, a great many variables involved in the healing process. This is particularly true when praying in faith for healing. No formula for success can be offered with any absolute guarantee — despite the fact that there are those who would suggest there is and that if a person follows their particular teaching, the outcome is assured. In all honesty, however, all that can be given are some general guidelines which come from experience and which have proved to be helpful when praying.

While these guidelines are based on sound principles and contain some factors which are essential for prayer, there is no assumption that the desired outcome is guaranteed if the guidelines are followed. Prayer simply does not work like that. Faith for healing, in the sense that it is used in this book, must always be in God and not in our ability to pray in some supposedly correct way. For this reason, it is important neither to make any assumptions when praying for someone to be healed, nor to place too much emphasis on the outcome of the prayer in advance, but simply to be prepared to pray and see what happens.

Prayer itself takes many forms. Most of the prayers we pray tend to be spontaneous outbursts, either expressions of praise or cries for help in time of need. Very little thought is given to this sort of prayer or its outcome. However, prayer for healing is generally much more deliberate than that and involves a lot of thought and preparation. Prayer for healing usually occurs in response to a felt need of one's own or a request by someone else. In both instances, the decision to pray for healing is generally a well-considered one and has a desired outcome in mind.

When considering what to pray for and how to pray, there are some general principles and guidelines which have proved to be helpful and from which we can learn, without having to slavishly follow them. However, some things are essential.

For instance, prayer for healing is an act of faith.

I have already said quite a lot about the nature of faith in this book and I have no intention of repeating it at length here, except to state again that it is important in healing prayer for faith to be *focussed outside of the self* and onto the One who is believed to have the power to heal.

It is also important for healing always to have in mind the *desired outcome* of the prayer, while remaining realistic about the present circumstances, and to reinforce faith with positive attitudes.

Faith must also include the *possibility of the unexpected* occurring in the form of a miracle. Therefore, it is important when praying for healing to expect the unexpected, even if it does not always happen.

It is always much easier to pray for healing in a group where there is the encouragement of others, than when alone. Of course, there will be times when individuals have no choice in the matter and will have to pray alone, either for themselves or for others. However, whether praying in a group for healing or when praying alone, the general guidelines are much the same.

The only major differences relate to the way the person praying deals with those things which emerge during the prayer time. If they concern the person praying, then one approach to dealing with them will have to be taken; if they concern the person being prayed for, another approach will need to be taken. These differences will become clear in the remainder of this chapter and in the next.

DISCOVERING THE DIFFERENT STAGES
OF PERSONAL PRAYER

When praying by yourself, a pattern of prayer usually begins to emerge after a while. It does not take a great deal of discernment to realise that this pattern generally falls into a logical sequence which indicates a number of different stages of prayer.

These stages will often occur naturally, though not all of them will necessarily be present on any given occasion. I have found the following framework a helpful way of understanding and applying these various stages of prayer to healing. They are as applicable to group prayer as they are to individual prayer.

❑ First, spend time in faith-building

When praying for oneself, it is important to spend some time in some faith-building activity. There are many appropriate ways of doing this and it is largely up to individuals to discover ones which suit them best.

Some people choose to do this by reading about the God in whom they are putting their trust and by speaking directly to him in words of adoration or thanksgiving. Sometimes, this will include an affirmation of the relationship which exists between the person praying and God, or an expression of how they feel about being loved by him. Others do it by singing or listening to music. Others, again, do it by various means of meditation which focus on the character of God and his goodness.

The purpose of these faith-building activities is to enable those who are praying to develop an attitude towards God whereby they feel confident enough to entrust him with their requests and have a reasonable expectation about the outcome.

❏ Second, spend time on focussing inwards

After preparing themselves in this way, those praying by themselves will often focus inwards. The awareness of their inner being may result in a deeply felt need to expose their inner lives to God and a desire to have him cleanse them of anything they have thought, said or done which is contrary to their belief system. This is sometimes accompanied by remorse and is an ideal way for people to rid themselves of any impediment in their lives to the healing they hope to receive.

The cleansing which takes place in this way is sometimes expressed in tears. It is often referred to as forgiveness and is the result of confession. If confession is made to another human being, rather than to God, it tends to lack the same feeling of assurance about the cleansed which accompanies confession to God and is therefore usually less cathartic as an experience and consequently less valuable in the healing process.

❑ Third, spend time in 'quietening down'

Before proceeding with the prayer, it is helpful to have a time of silence. This is not a time of meditation, but a time of quietening down in order to allow communion to take place between your spirit and God's Spirit.

It is not unusual for such reflections as the following to surface during this time which prove to be helpful when praying for healing:

a. *Repressed memories.* I have known people to become aware of long-repressed memories during this time of silence. If this happens, they can be offered to God for healing straightaway. However, if the memories which surface during the time of silence cause distress in any way, it is best to see a qualified counsellor as soon as possible.

b. *Revelations.* Some people have reported seeing or imagining pictures in their mind which prove to be significant in helping them know how to pray or what to pray for. Others recall encouraging words, particularly from some inspirational source such as the Bible, which have helped them believe for healing. Still others have reported a strong urge to rectify past wrongs, particularly in relationships, before proceeding.

If any of these revelations emerge when praying for yourself, it is relatively easy to deal with them in a helpful, positive way by choosing the appropriate means of doing so.

However, if any of them relate to the person being prayed for, it is best not to interfere unless permission to do so has been given and it seems to be the wise course of action. It may be better to use that information in your own prayers, or to pray that God will reveal it to the person concerned, rather than to confront the other person with it.

There is always the possibility that you may have got the wrong message. It is also possible that it may have come from your own subconscious mind rather than from a supernatural source — in which case it may be relevant to you rather than to the other person, or simply have no relevance at all. Whichever it is, it may cause more harm than healing to raise such matters with the person being prayed for.

It is always wise to be tentative when reporting such revelations, given that it is easy to get them wrong. Care must be exercised with revelations of this nature.

c. *Communing with God.* If nothing of any significance comes into your mind during the time of silence, it does not matter, as long as the period of silence makes you more aware of God and of your relationship of faith to him. This in itself will help you be more single-minded about what you are praying for and more open to him in the rest of the prayer.

If something significant does arise in the time of silence, it is important to deal with it in an appropriate way. This could include checking it out, praying it through, or seeking help in understanding and resolving whatever has come to light.

❑ **Fourth, be aware of the reality of the problem and the desired outcome of the prayer**

Some people do this visually; others do it conceptually. It is of no great consequence how it is done as long as the process of looking beyond the present condition to the desired healing does not deny reality.

There is a fine balance between present reality and future hope when praying for healing. However, with a goal or outcome firmly in mind, it is much easier to pray for it and to eliminate any negative thoughts which may be counterproductive to positive faith. It is essential when praying in this way to concentrate on the positives and to reinforce any signs of improvement in the condition being prayed for with thoughts and words of faith and hope, such as a simple expression of thanks for what has happened and a restatement of the desired outcome.

Responding to positive changes like this will affect the way the rest of the prayer is prayed by keeping it realistic and positive. This stage of the prayer is often the hardest, as it involves faith as well as a positive mindset.

❏ Fifth, clearly verbalise the request

After this it is simply a matter of proceeding with the prayer, by restating your faith in God and making your request as simply and directly as possible. Some people like to repeat their request over and over again. Others find it helpful to conclude with silence or to verbalise a simple statement of thanks in anticipation that the prayer has been heard and will be answered in some way.

The conviction that an answer will come is in keeping with the sort of prayer which is predicated on faith in God and which trusts him for a response without prescribing the outcome.

It is not wrong to pray repetitively, but it may be more helpful when continuing to pray for a particular need, to pray on separate occasions rather than over and over again on the same occasion. The way this is done should incorporate the principles of reality, faith and positive reinforcement as described previously.

However, it is important to continue praying for the need until it is clear that the prayer should stop. An indication of this would be that the need has been met, a more appropriate answer than the one hoped for has been given, or even that the prayer has failed altogether to bring the desired outcome.

9

How group prayer can be part of the healing process

WHEN PRAYING WITH OTHERS FOR SOMEONE to be healed, the principles and guidelines mentioned above are much the same. It is important to engage in some faith-building activity in the group; to focus inwards in order to give the individual members of the group the opportunity of dealing with anything in their own lives which needs cleansing; to quieten down so that spiritual communion with God may take place and those praying may be aware of any special way in which God may be revealing something significant to them; to face the reality of the problem and the to look beyond it to the desired outcome by verbalising the request.

However, a much more powerful dynamic seems to be at work when a group prays for someone than when an individual prays alone, especially if that person is present. While it is hard to define what this dynamic is except in spiritual terms, it is important not to abuse it in any way nor to impose unnecessary burdens on those being prayed for.

To avoid these dangers, it is necessary to have some understanding of the way in which healing prayer works within a group and how to respond to what is happening at the time. The following has proved helpful to me and to many others:

❏ Prepare for prayer

Always make every effort to ensure that the person being prayed for is comfortable, at ease and feeling under no pressure to perform. The very nature of group prayer often generates anxiety and high expectation to do the right thing. There is a sense in which there is no right thing, so the person being prayed for needs to be reassured that they are amongst friends, that everyone is equally involved in the process and that as the only reason they have come together as a group is to pray in faith, there is no need for anxiety, since the outcome depends on God and not on them.

The faith-building and self-disclosure aspects of prayer may be done individually by those taking part in the prayer before the group prayer begins, or they may be part of the group activity. In most cases, the first option is preferable, as it is both good preparation and less threatening for the person being prayed for. Besides, if they are done beforehand, the danger of diverting attention from the person being prayed for to those doing the praying is avoided.

It is nearly always helpful to begin with some group acknowledgement of God and a reaffirmation of faith in him to heal. This can be done with a simple prayer, a song, an encouraging reading or by sharing some faith-building words from past experience. This helps to galvanise the faith of the group and to ensure that everyone has the same purpose in mind.

This part of the prayer time is best kept short so as not to build an emotionally charged atmosphere which may distract the participants in the prayer from what is really taking place.

❑ Know what you are praying for

After a short faith-building activity, it is important to get some accurate information about the nature of the problem of the person being prayed for and the hoped-for outcome.

This information is best obtained by asking the person directly and matter-of-factly. A prayer time like this is *not* a counselling session; it is *not* an excuse to give a moralistic or spiritual lecture to the person being prayed for; and you do *not* have any right to correct their expectations, impose guilt upon them by suggesting lack of faith, or subject them to any spiritual or emotional pressure because of their problem. I need to stress this, because all of these things happen regularly in healing prayer and nearly always cause spiritual or emotional distress. I can only guess at the harm it does to a person's physical condition.

At this stage of the prayer, you only have the right to ask for and receive the information you need to help you pray. That information, if it is to be helpful, must reflect their present circumstances and not deny reality. It must also express a desired outcome of the prayer. For healing prayer to be effective when praying in a group, it must take its lead initially from the person being prayed for or from God, not from those who are there to pray. There will be time later for supporters to take some initiative.

❑ Generate a positive faith

When the person being prayed for has expressed their need and their hopes, those who are praying must try to look beyond the need and focus their mind on God. Together or individually, they must try to eliminate any negative thoughts about the condition they are praying for and give their full attention to the desired outcome. They can gain support for this from those present by verbalising their faith and by using positive language.

They should never deny the reality of the situation, but try to look beyond it to the God in whom they trust and from whom they are seeking help. This can be done by referring in their prayers to the desired outcome.

❑ **Give a time of silence for God to be involved**
When the person being prayed for in the group becomes comfortable about taking this approach to prayer, it is not wise to start praying straightaway, but to wait a while in silence. This time of silence gives an opportunity for communion between the spirit of those praying and those being prayed for, and God's Spirit. It also allows God to be involved in the process of praying by making his presence felt in the following ways, as well as those I mentioned in the chapter on praying alone.

a. *It can be helpful for some of those praying to place their hands lightly on the person being prayed for,* but only with their permission and in a way which does not violate their personal space or cause embarrassment. There is no need to place hands on the head of the person being prayed for as practised in some circles, although as a symbolic gesture it can sometimes prove to be helpful in generating faith or imparting a feeling of acceptance to the person being prayed for.

b. *Any cues should be taken from the person being prayed for.* I have been present when those being prayed for have begun to show signs of being in touch with emotional trauma or distress, or to express their emotions in a demonstrative way. When this happens, it is always best to ask the person who is reacting in this way what is happening for them and to pray accordingly.

The cue for prayer should always come from the person being prayed for, not from the intuition, past experience or presumption of those praying.

c. *Do not jump to conclusions about what may appear to be happening during the time of silence.* It is very easy to be misled by what may appear to be happening during the time of silence. People react in different ways during prayer. Often, their reactions are related to something which is going on inside them, whether spiritually, emotionally or spiritually, and it is very easy for someone looking on to misinterpret them.

For instance, it is not uncommon to see physical reactions such as shaking, swaying or tears. These reactions may be nothing more than a physical response to the emotionally charged atmosphere in which the prayer is taking place or may even be a form of self-hypnosis. They may also be little more than play-acting — the person involved only doing what they think is expected of them because of some bogus comments they have heard somewhere in relation to healing prayer.

However, there may equally be an emotional

release associated with a sudden awareness of re-pressed memories. Because of these and many other possibilities, it is best not to jump to conclusions about what is happening, but to ask the person being prayed for what is going on for them and what meaning they themselves give to it.

Even with the best of intentions, it is very easy to make mistakes and pray for the wrong thing unless you check out any reactions which may occur during the prayer time with the person being prayed for and not make any assumptions about them.

I remember praying in a group for a young woman who, during this part of the prayer, began to show on her face all the physical signs of demon possession, at least according to popular mythology. Some of those praying for her immediately wanted to start a process of exorcism. I refused to let them but, instead, asked the woman what was happening for her.

She explained that she was in touch with a very painful memory from childhood. This memory had obviously been repressed until the time we began to pray. The expression on her face and the grotesque distortions of her body were manifestations of the pain associated with that memory. Once that fact became clear, it determined the way we prayed for her that night.

To have proceeded on the assumption that she was demon-possessed would have been disastrous, because it suggested an explanation and cure for her problem which was not correct, while completely missing an important area of her life which needed resolving before her healing could take place.

A young man we prayed for at a small gathering on one occasion began to weep bitterly during the time of silence. Because of what had happened just prior to this, some of those praying assumed that they were tears of remorse for something he had done wrong and began to pray accordingly. I stopped them and asked him what the tears were about.

They proved to be tears of regret for his lost childhood which he associated with his father's death when he was three years old. The grief he was experiencing made the prayer very different from the way it would have gone if it had proceeded along the lines of the first assumption.

d. *Be open in the silence to direct revelation.* There are many times I can recall when one or more of those who are praying in a group for another person will have a picture come into their mind, or will have a thought or even some words which they think may have some relevance to the situation. Again, it is unwise to make any assumptions about this. These things need to be tested by asking the person being prayed for if they have any meaning for them.

It is always wise to do this tentatively and never imply that you have a special revelation, because you may be wrong or, worse still, you may unwittingly put pressure on the person being prayed for to agree with something which is not true for them. Besides, the picture or thoughts when verbalised may touch a chord which the person being prayed for might prefer to deal with in private, either because of its intimacy or the embarrassment associated with it, or for some other legitimate reason. It is always necessary to respect the integrity of the person being prayed for and never to embarrass them in any way.

Having said that, there are times when direct revelation occurs and we need to be sensitive to these. I was once asked to pray for a young man who was suffering from a disfiguring dermatitis which seemed resistant to all medical treatment. As I prayed with some others for him, a picture of a child falling off a tricycle came into my mind. The picture also included a young woman turning her back on the child and ignoring him. I tentatively described this picture to the young man and asked whether it meant anything to him. When he reacted angrily and said that it did not, I simply prayed for him to be healed of his physical condition, assuming I had made a mistake.

By chance I saw that same young man a few months later and his skin was perfectly clear. When I asked him what had happened, he reminded me of the picture I had when praying for him. He said that he didn't know why he had reacted so angrily but, when he told his mother about it, she began to cry.

She told him that the picture described an incident which had taken place at a time when she was very depressed and didn't know how to cope with an active young son. Ever since that period in her life, she had felt a distance between her and her son which she didn't understand or knew how to resolve. As they talked, they were able to resolve the difficulty in their relationship, and not long after that his dermatitis began to clear up.

There is nothing particularly remarkable about the connection between this young man's dermatitis and the emotional trauma in his childhood. What is remarkable is the way in which the key to dealing with this connection was unlocked through a picture which came into my mind when we were silently communing with God. The picture may have meant nothing at the time, but it proved to be the key to this young man's physical healing.

On numerous occasions, I can recall words have come into the minds of those praying which have proved to be helpful when shared tentatively with the person being prayed for. As in every other aspect of praying with others, words have to be tested in relation to the person being prayed for to see if they have any meaning for them.

It is very difficult to predict what that meaning might be. More often than not, the words which come into mind during a time of prayer will have their origin in some inspiring reading that the person who has them has engaged in in the past. These are sometimes recalled accurately from the source or quoted in a general way. They often prove to be helpful, encouraging or comforting.

However, sometimes the words have no known origin and may even be humorous or lacking any meaning to the person who speaks them out. In these cases, extreme caution needs to be exercised when verbalising them and the possibility that they mean nothing at all in relation to the person being prayed for needs to be kept in mind.

I remember vividly having some humorous words about a particular breakfast cereal come to mind which seemed at the time to be totally unrelated to anything which was happening during the time of prayer I was engaged in. Never- the-less, when I verbalised them with some hesitation, the words seemed to have immediate significance to the person being prayed for. She had asked for prayer for a particular set of symptoms which were not responding to treatment. However, the words about the breakfast cereal somehow managed to make the person aware of the way she was consuming unreasonable quantities of it as a way of coping with the emotional difficulties she was experiencing at the time.

As a result of this revelation, she was able to tell her doctor the full story of what was going on. It turned out that the particular breakfast cereal she had been eating had a very high salt content which had been causing the unusual symptoms. From that time on, her physical healing was a simple matter of the correct treatment. Her emotional healing took place through counselling and further prayer.

❑ Verbalise your requests

After a suitable time of silence has elapsed, it is time to pray for the healing itself. If nothing has arisen in the time of silence, this prayer will be straight-forward. It needs to be positive in the sense that I have described it in the earlier chapter on praying by oneself and it will of necessity concentrate on the desired outcome.

It is during this phase of the prayer that there is usually opportunity for those praying to take some initiative in deciding how to pray and what to pray for. However, I again urge that this phase of the prayer be conducted in accordance with what has already taken place in the prayer time and in response to the wishes of the person being prayed for.

It is important when praying for someone who is present in a group to recognise that there is not always an obvious answer to prayer. Those being prayed for need to be prepared for this possibility in a way which does not undermine their faith. The only way of doing this is to be realistic about healing and not raise false expectations. A person being prayed for needs to be aware that not everyone who is prayed for is healed, that some people find a different form of healing from the one that they originally sought and that others find only partial healing.

Despite this, however, they need to be instructed that there is every reason to hope for a miracle, given the character of God, the nature of faith and the power of the mind. With proper preparation and understanding of the healing process, it is possible to approach healing positively and openly, and to trust God no matter what may result.

❑ Make a long-term commitment

One of the big mistakes that is often made when praying for someone to be healed is to abandon them if the healing does not take place immediately. Even those who are healed may find that this is only the beginning of a long process. It is important to provide aftercare for those who have been healed and not to abandon them.

The need for long-term commitment and patience when praying for people to be healed has been clearly demonstrated throughout this book. If a person is abandoned because the healing does not come in the way or at the time hoped for, it is likely that they will suffer further distress of a spiritual or emotional kind to add to their troubles.

Any involvement in praying for people must include a commitment to their total well-being. This does not mean providing all things to all people, but it does require a willingness to encourage those seeking healing to find the full range of help and support they need to be made whole.

It is necessary, when praying for healing, to recognise that those who are not healed may need to be referred to others with more specialised skills. Neither the person being prayed for, nor those doing the praying should feel any sense of failure in this, for prayer is only part of the total healing process.

It is important when praying for someone to be healed to remember that there is no prayer formula which guarantees absolute success. The points which are set out above do not constitute such a formula, but are merely some of the insights I have gained from my experience of praying for healing.

My hope is that they might help others circumvent unnecessary mistakes when praying for healing. All, some or none of the above may be present in a given prayer session. It may take an entirely different course altogether — it does not matter. The important thing is to have the courage

to pray for ourselves and others when confronted
with the need to do so.

A FINAL WORD

Healing is about the whole person — body, mind
and spirit. There are many ways of achieving healing and many variables in the healing process. With
all the wonderful advances in scientific medicine, the
exploration of the mind-body connection and the
serious consideration that is being given to some
alternative forms of healing, there is still a tendency
to overlook the spiritual dimension of healing. This
neglect has enabled a number of dubious religious
systems to seek to fill the gap. However, there is an
acceptable source of spiritual comfort and help available to those who come from traditional Western
backgrounds which is compatible with their beliefs.
That resource is prayer.

Prayer for healing is a precious resource which is
often overlooked or misunderstood. It is a spiritual
resource which depends on faith in God. God is
external to the self and yet wonderfully accessible
through prayer. By any definition, his power is
greater than ours and he is therefore capable of
performing miracles. It is the hope of a miraculous
intervention in our lives which encourages us to
pray for healing and utilise the natural healing processes of the body however we can.

My own experience of praying in faith for healing is predicated on the relationship I have to God through believing in Jesus. I firmly believe that, while many of the benefits of faith which I have described in this book are available through other belief systems, the full range of benefits is only available through the Christian faith. Because I relate to God through faith in Jesus, I dare to pray for healing in the way I do — and to hope for a miracle.

However, my faith is not affected by the outcome of my prayers because, although it is firmly rooted in this life, it looks beyond the present to a world yet to come. My ultimate hope lies in that world, not in this one.

Appendix:
The darker side of healing

ONE OF THE MOST DIFFICULT and contentious areas of healing to deal with is that of the nature of evil and the effect it can have on our well-being, for it inevitably touches on the associated questions of whether or not demonic possession is a possible diagnosis of illness and, if so, how you deal with it.

The difficulty relating to this is twofold. First, there is a tendency on the part of some groups, particularly those of a more fundamentalist religious persuasion, to want to attribute a demonic cause to almost every known illness, whether of a physical or mental nature, and to treat it with a crude form of exorcism. Not only are such approaches simplistic in the extreme, but can be very dangerous in the effect they have on those who are subjected to such diagnosis and treatment. They have even been known to cause the death of the sufferer, despite their good intentions.

Second, there are those whose more rationalistic approach causes them to overlook this possibility of demonic possession and so they fail to effect healing in a person so afflicted.

Both these positions need to be avoided, for there are times when the possession syndrome is a legitimate and genuine diagnosis of a problem and needs to be taken seriously. In my experience, however, the number of such cases is relatively small — somewhere in the order of three to five per cent of those who present themselves for counselling or prayer while exhibiting some behaviour patterns of symptoms which could superficially be interpreted as demonic. When a genuine case of demonic possession is uncovered, it needs to be dealt with by those who have some experience in this sort of activity and are prepared for the emotional and spiritual cost involved.

In order to avoid a superficial diagnosis in this area and the possibility of causing more harm than good in trying to treat a misdiagnosed problem, I suggest that the possibility of demonic possession be considered as the diagnosis of last resort. By that I mean that it is wise not to assume that a presenting problem has a demonic cause, but rather work through the other possibilities first. Where there is no obvious cause of a problem, or where the problem is a natural consequence of living in a world which is full of hazards which cause illness and contribute to a lack of well-being, this process of diagnosis may take some time.

However, unless you can be certain of the diagnosis, it is always wisest to pray in a general way until there is some more obvious reason to pray more specifically. When this is necessary, due care needs to be taken and the whole process properly supervised.

Bibliography

AT ANY GIVEN TIME, literally hundreds of books on the subject of healing are available from any large bookshop. They cover every conceivable aspect of healing and are written from many different perspectives. However, not all of them are helpful and some of them have even proved to be misleading.

With this in mind, I have had a great deal of trouble selecting even the following few books from those which I have read on the subject of this book.

On the whole, the books listed below are written for the general reader rather than the specialist, have something significant or substantial to say about the subject, have been relatively recently published, and are readily available either from bookshops or in libraries. They all approach the subject of healing from a holistic perspective and are based on good research or sound experience. However, that does not mean that I would endorse all of what they are saying, particularly those which have a different spiritual agenda or value system to my own.

I would urge caution and discernment in reading them, and a willingness to learn and adapt rather than follow slavishly what is written in them. For any whose interest is roused and who would like to pursue these issues further, most of the books listed have excellent bibliographies.

❏ Joan Borysenko with Larry Rothstew, *Minding the Body, Mending the Mind*, Addison-Wesley, 1987
Joan Borysenko was responsible, with others, for establishing the Mind-Body Clinic in Boston, USA. She brings her scientific research, clinical practice and personal experience together in this book in a way which clearly demonstrates the healing power of the mind. It is interesting to note the emphasis she gives to spiritual understanding in her own experience of healing and in her clinical work.

❏ Morton T. Kelsey, *Healing and Christianity*, Harper and Row, 1973
This book claims to be the first comprehensive history of sacramental healing in the Christian Church from biblical times to the present. In it, Morton Kelsey offers a balanced and dispassionate assessment of the foundations of the healing ministry in the church from the earliest times, and offers a biblical, theological and psychological framework within which to understand and practice healing today from a Christian perspective.

❏ Melvin Kenmer, *The Trouble with Medicine*, ABC Books, 1993
This book, which is linked to a television series of the same title, examines a number of different approaches to healing being taken in various parts of the world from a holistic perspective and offers some helpful insights into the work of some well-known practitioners of this aspect of healing, such as Dr Bernie Siegal.

It also deals with some of the problems associated with the costs of modern scientific medicine, and the failure and futility of looking for a so-called 'magic bullet' as a panacea for healing various illnesses. The book also discusses in a very helpful and readable way a number of other important questions being asked about the practice of medicine today.

❑ Bill Moyers, *Healing and the Mind*, Doubleday, 1993

Like the last book, this one is linked to a TV series of the same name. As such, the material is presented in an easily understood and entertaining way, while at the same time imparting important information on the latest research and practice in this area from different places around the world.

A very helpful book indeed for anyone who is looking for an easy introduction to this area of medicine and its application to the process of healing the whole person.

❑ Donald Norfolk, *Think Well, Feel Great: 7 B-Attitudes That Can Change Your Life*, Michael Joseph, 1990

This is a critique of scientific medicine when it seeks to heal the body without duly considering the mind. The author develops a philosophy of health and healing which includes the whole person. He develops the importance of certain attitudes in maintaining health, attitudes which he refers to as commitment, calmness, confidence, conviviality, optimism, cheerfulness, contentment and the integrated personality. He gives some helpful advice on how these attitudes can be developed.

❑ Robert Ornstein and David Sobel, *The Healing Brain:*

A Radical New Approach to Health Care, Macmillan, 1988

The authors of this book state that they draw on recent research in neurology and brain chemistry to show that the most important ally in the healing process is the patient. 'They demonstrate how the brain controls the immune system, regulates pain and uses our emotions for better health. And they explain why unrelated psychological and social factors, such as the strength of human relationships, increases one's resistance to disease.'

These words from the dustjacket of the book state exactly what the book has to offer in our understanding of healing in terms of the mind-body connection and how the brain can be harnessed in a preventative, not just corrective way, in the healing process.

❑ M. Scott Peck, *The Road Less Travelled: A New Psychology of Love, Traditional Values and Spiritual Growth*, Century Paperbacks, 1987

This book has proved to be both influential and helpful in the quest for spiritual healing and wholeness. Written by a practising psychiatrist who is not afraid to use his own journey through life as well as his clinical experience to support his position and encourage spiritual and emotional growth in others, it offers some practical guidelines along with a sound theoretical underpinning for what is said.

Scott Peck has a lot to say about love and resolving difficulties in relationships, and is well aware of the important connection between the emotions and the body for a sense of well-being.

❑ Martin L. Rossman, M.D., *Healing Yourself: A*

Step-by-Step Program for Better Health Through Imagery, An Institute for the Advancement of Health Book, Walker and Company, 1987

Written by a medical doctor, this book looks at an increasingly popular form of self-healing or faith healing through imagery. It is a self-help book, which sets out to teach a program of relaxation and meditation which may lead to inner peace and better health.

The program is supported by research in psychology, neurology and immunology and purports to have had widespread success. It is another way of applying the mind-body connection to healing. Some people may find that a number of the suggestions made here will need to be modified or adapted in order to avoid conflict with their religious or philosophical framework. However, this is not difficult to do.

❑ Bernie S. Siegel, M.D., *Love, Medicine and Miracles*, Rider and Co. Ltd, 1986

Bernie Siegel, Assistant Clinical Professor of Surgery at Yale Medical School, draws on his clinical experience to show the importance of attitudes in the healing process, including the attitude of patients towards their illnesses and the attitude of doctors towards their patients. He makes an important link between attitudes generally and hope, and urges patients to be in control of their illness. He suggests that right attitudes may prolong life beyond medical expectation.

❑ O. Carl Simenton, with Stephanie Matthews-Simenton and James L. Creighton, *Getting Well Again*, Bantam Books, 1986

This was one of the earliest books to popularise the developing interest in the mind-body connection in healing amongst medical practitioners at the time. It deals with the importance of such issues as lifestyle, proper relationships (including the healing power of forgiveness) and meditation, as well as proper medical care in the treatment and cure of cancer patients.

There has been a large number of books since then which have developed these ideas in practice, often related to either personal experience of healing or a particular philosophy or lifestyle. These books are available in almost any bookshop in great abundance, and have proved to be both inspiring and helpful to many for various reasons.

❑ Harold Taylor, *Sent to Heal: A Handbook to Christian Healing*, Order of St Luke, 44 Arum Crescent, Ringwood, Victoria 3134, Australia

This, as the title suggests, is a handbook, primarily written for the members of the Order of St Luke, a society which exists to promote the ministry of healing in the churches.

The book is written for the general reader and deals with a number of the biblical and practical issues related to healing. It gathers together in one volume the information contained in a number of pamphlets and booklets previously published separately by the Order of St Luke and for this, if for no other reason, it is a helpful addition to our understanding of healing in its widest sense as practised in the Christian church.

❑ John Wilkinson, *Health and Healing: Studies in New Testament Principles and Practice*, The Handset Press, 1980

This is a scholarly, though very readable set of studies which, while not excluding the Old Testament from consideration, sets out a New Testament framework for understanding the healing ministry. It deals thoughtfully with some of the difficult passages concerning healing in the New Testament and concludes with some comments on the way in which the healing commission given by Jesus to his disciples may be applied in the church today.

*   *   *

There are numerous popular books on the market which explore the mind-body connection in healing from an intuitive, scientific, medical or religious viewpoint. While many of these offer little more than a smorgasbord of New Age philosophy, alternative medicine or self-help therapies, some have made a significant if somewhat simplistic contribution to our understanding of healing.

The following interpretations of healing or wholeness from a Christian perspective have proved to be influential in recent years:

❑ Jim Glennon, *Your Healing is Within You*, Hodder and Stoughton, 1978

❑ Francis MacNutt, *Healing*, Ave Maria Press/ Notre Dame, 1974

❑ Norman Vincent Peale, *The Power of Positive Thinking*, Cedar Press, 1953

❑ John Wimber, *Power Healing*, Hodder and Stoughton, 1986